The
Burden Made Light

By
ALFRED DOERFFLER
St. Louis, Mo.

St. Louis, Mo.
CONCORDIA PUBLISHING HOUSE
1937

TO MY SHUT-INS

Meditations and Prayers for Sick, Convalescents, Invalids, and Afflicted Seeking Comfort, Strength, Encouragement, Hope, and Peace in the Glorious Gospel of Jesus Christ, Our Savior and Friend

"Come unto Me, all ye that labor and are heavy laden, and I will give you rest. Take My yoke upon you and learn of Me; for I am meek and lowly in heart; and ye shall find rest unto your souls. For My yoke is easy, and My burden is light."

God sometimes shuts the door and shuts us in,
  That He may speak, perchance through grief or pain,
And softly, heart to heart, above the din,
  May tell some precious thought to us again.

God sometimes shuts the door and keeps us still
  That so our feverish haste or deep unrest
Beneath His gentle touch may quiet, till
  He whispers what our weary hearts love best.

CONTENTS

Contents

The Book of Books

Thy Word have I hidden in my heart. — Ps. 119, 11.

The greatest treasure in the world is the Bible. The Bible is the oldest book, and yet it is the most up-to-date book because it fits your condition and mine. There is no other book in the world which has directed the thoughts of men and influenced the human race like this Book.

God claims this Book, the Bible, as His own. God tells us that He has given this Book by inspiration. With the word *inspire* God means to tell us that He has given the Bible to the human race by a special, unique inbreathing. This method of inspiring is limited to certain men, to the prophets in the Old Testament and the apostles in the New Testament.

These writers were moved to speak by the Holy Ghost. "Holy men of God spake as they were moved by the Holy Ghost," 2 Pet. 1, 21. David says: "The Spirit of God spake by me, and His Word was in my tongue," 2 Sam. 23, 2.

God claims that all of this Book, every word, is His own. Therefore the writers did not include their own ideas and took no credit for any part of the Bible as their own. The Bible does not merely contain the Word of God, but *is* His Word.

God claims that nothing else is authoritative in religious matters. All that God reveals to man He has spoken through this Word. Therefore the Bible is complete. We are not to expect any new revelations. All that we need to know is found in the Bible.

Therefore this Word is final. Whatever the Bible states is unchangeable and infallible. God has nothing more to say. Therefore the Bible speaks with authority on all questions of doctrine and morals.

This Bible is *your* Book. "Thy Word have I hid in my heart." As you are a Christian, this Treasure Book is to be in your home, in your life, and in your heart. This Book serves as a touchstone. From this Bible you will learn to know what is true and what is not true, what you should do and what you must not do, what you are to believe and what you are not to believe.

This Book serves you as a guide. It leads you into the narrow way and guards you against the pitfalls of sin. It is a lamp that lights up the way, the beacon-light that points to the harbor of heaven.

This Book serves you also as a companion. It cheers you as you meet with disappointments and failures. It assures you that the Lord is your Shepherd and that Jesus is your Savior. As companion it comforts you in your sorrows and dries your tears. As companion it fills you with hope. There is no condition in life in which it has not a message for you.

That is why the Bible is a real Treasure Book, and only God could give it to us. Therefore hide it in your heart; that is, read it, believe it, love it. Follow its instructions and hold fast to it as God's message to you.

Prayer

Lord God, merciful Father, I thank Thee that Thou hast revealed Thyself unto me in the Scriptures and hast made me wise unto salvation through this glorious Gospel, which can save to the uttermost. Let this Thy Word be hid in my heart that I may love it and read it daily and find in it strength and comfort and help. Let nothing in the world be dearer to me. May I see in it the one thing needful. Grant that no one will have power over me and cause me to question the truthfulness of Thy inspired Word, but that I may believe with childlike faith every word that Thou hast spoken.

Let this Word reach the ends of the earth, and let it bring peace to thousands even as it brings peace and hope to my heart. Forgive me every sin and keep me and all mine in Thy saving grace. May the study of Thy Word be our daily delight! I ask this because of Him who is the living Word from heaven, Christ Jesus, my Lord. Amen.

Greater than Mother-Love

Can a woman forget her sucking child that she should not have compassion on the son of her womb? Yet, they may forget, yet will I not forget thee. — *Is. 49, 15.*

God uses here the love of a mother to illustrate His love. Mother-love is a picture of God's love, great and glorious, but not so wonderful. The rose painted on the canvas is never as beautiful as the rose-bud in the garden. Yet God sees fit to compare His own love with that of a mother. As He seeks to demonstrate to sinful man how much He loves us, God tells us that He loves us *more* than a mother.

Can a mother forget her sucking child? Yea, she may forget. Mothers have abandoned their children. It is in-human for a mother to forget. But even though she may forget, yet God never forgets us. God's love never ceases to flow toward the sinner. God's love never lets us go. That is why Paul says in Romans 8: "I am persuaded that neither death, nor life, nor angels, nor principalities, nor powers, nor things present, nor things to come, nor height, nor depth, nor any other creature shall be able to separate us from the love of God which is in Christ Jesus, our Lord."

No matter how great our troubles and how trying our sufferings, God knows, and He cares. God always brings to pass the events of our lives in such a way that in the end we praise Him for His wisdom and grace. Therefore we should delight in waiting upon the Lord and diligently study His promises as they are found in His Word. Clinging to these promises, we cannot despair. God, who is from everlasting to everlasting, knoweth our downsitting and our uprising and is acquainted with all our ways. Therefore it is better to trust in the Lord than to put our confidence in man. Each morning we hope anew because the Lord of hosts is with us and the God of Jacob is our Refuge.

Let us, then, write into our discouraged and anxious hearts this promise of God: "Yet will I not forget thee."

Prayer

Thou hast promised to me, gracious Father, Thy presence day after day. Therefore I lift up mine eyes unto Thee, from whom cometh my help. Thou knowest all things and art acquainted with all my ways and with all my struggles and problems. With these I come into Thy throne-room, petitioning Thee to give me strength and help. Show me, O Lord, the way that I should go. Guide me and keep me safely every hour of the day.

Give to me the grace to remember daily Thy great, wonderful love toward me and all mankind, which is so great that Thou didst send Thine only-begotten Son to redeem me that I might be Thine own. In Thy tender love blot out all my sins and remember them no more. Fill me with Thy heavenly peace.

Bless this our home with Thy divine presence. Let each one of us know that Thou art very near. Fill each with contentment and patience and love. Remove from us all the worries and cares that want to beset us. We ask this because of Him who in His great love laid down His life for us all, Christ Jesus. Amen.

The First Principles of Prayer

Whatsoever ye shall ask the Father in My name, He will give it you. Hitherto have ye asked nothing in My name: ask, and ye shall receive that your joy may be full. — *John 16, 23. 24.*

The Scriptures urge us to pray. Yet many complain that their prayers remain unanswered. They have not obtained the results for which they were looking. Has God failed in His promises? Are Jesus' words empty and meaningless? Never. If there is no answer to our prayer, the fault lies with us. Therefore we ought to search the Scriptures diligently and like the disciples ask the Lord to teach us how to pray. God has laid down certain principles of prayer which, if we follow them, assure us God's answer to every petition that we make.

First we are to pray according to the will of God. One who prays must never forget that by the nature of the case He must recognize that God is Lord of all things. Therefore prayer dare not be a dictating to the almighty and all-wise God, telling Him what He must do and how He must do it. God knows better than we what the future has in store for us. Often we think that we cannot live unless we have our way. Here is a young woman who deeply loves a young man. They have a quarrel and part. She is heart-broken. She goes to God in prayer, asking that He would bring about a reconciliation. But they never make up, and she cannot understand why her prayer remained unanswered. Ten years later, however, she again meets this young man and then thanks God that she never married him. Therefore, as we go to God in prayer, asking Him to heal us, to give us daily bread, to give us the many things that we think we need for this life, let us always pray: If it be Thy will.

Secondly we are to pray in Jesus' name. Between us and God are mountains of sin. These sins must be removed before God will be inclined to listen with a friendly ear. But *we* cannot remove sin. We cannot go back into our yesterdays and live our life over. We cannot by the tears that we shed, wash away sin, just as little as our tears can mend the broken china. Jesus must remove our sins, and He has done this by the shedding of His holy, precious blood. Therefore in the name of Jesus we can approach the throne of God. If we come to God through Christ, we shall find a loving Father, who will hear our prayer and lift our burdens or give us strength to bear them.

Thirdly, we are to pray believing. Prayer should not

be done mechanically or automatically. It is not like drop-
ping a prayer in an automatic machine, and out comes
an answer. A prayer must come from the heart. We must
believe that God will answer. But in order that we may
pray with such a believing heart, the Holy Spirit must
dwell in us and give us this confidence and faith in God.

If we pray according to the will of God, in the name of
our Lord Jesus Christ, and with a faith created by the Holy
Spirit, we shall never complain of unanswered prayer. As
we ask, we shall receive, and joy shall fill our hearts.

Prayer

Lord, teach me to pray. As I pray, let Thy love and Thy
mercy shine into my heart. Cleanse me from every sin that my
heart may be a temple wherein Thou canst dwell. Give me faith
to believe Thy promises and to trust in Thy mercies.

Lord, Thou knowest all things and art acquainted with all my
problems. There is not a word upon my tongue but, Lord, Thou
knowest it altogether. I feel therefore my unworthiness, and yet
I need Thee. If Thou wilt not bless me, I perish; if Thou dost
not give me the needed strength, I shall go down in defeat;
if Thou dost not fill me with hope, I have nothing to which I can
cling. Therefore I come to Thee because Thou hast asked me
to come and seek Thy face and promised to watch over me every
moment of the day.

Bless our home. Grant that not one may go through the
day unforgiven. I approach Thee in this prayer, asking Thee
for pardon and guidance because of Him who taught me to pray,
Christ Jesus, my Savior. Amen.

The Call to Prayer

Let us therefore come boldly unto the Throne of Grace that
we may obtain mercy and find grace to help in the time of need.
Heb. 4, 16.

Here we have the call to prayer. The days of trouble
are days when we ought to pray often. In our distress we
learn to pray earnestly. The strongest men and the most

heroic women, the calmest and most unruffled, pray in the trying hours of life. Jesus Himself was a man of prayer.

But how can we who are sinful heed this call to prayer? It takes courage to face God as our transgressions come to our remembrance. We are undeserving of answered prayers. We dare to come because God's throne has become a Throne of Grace through our Lord Jesus Christ. Boldly we can come and make our petitions because the blood of Jesus Christ blots out all our sins and thus takes the dark lines out of the face of God.

We should come boldly. That means confidently. We dare to come confidently because God invites us to come when He says through His Son Jesus Christ: "Ask, and it shall be given you; . . . for every one that asketh, receiveth," Luke 11, 9. 10. Boldly means coming courageously. We are not afraid of God. We know that He will not smite us down or close the door upon us. Through our Lord Jesus Christ, God is friendly toward us and loves us with an undying love.

If we come boldly, in the name of Jesus, to the throne of God, we shall find mercy and help in the time of need. God is the Lord Almighty. With Him everything is possible. I do not know how He is going to answer prayer, but this I do know, that He does answer. To the penitent who comes pleading for mercy He gives full forgiveness. To the troubled who is being crushed under the burdens of the day He gives strength. To the sorrowing out of whose day the light has gone He brings hope. Whosoever comes will find that God is ever ready to listen to His plea.

Since God offers us such riches and blessings and gives us such promises, let us heed this call to prayer and day after day boldly come unto the Throne of Grace with all our sins, our burdens, and our troubles, confidently believing that we shall find help.

Prayer

To Thy throne-room I come, O Lord, seeking Thy divine help. Grant, I pray Thee, full remission of all my sins through Jesus Christ and take from me every worry and every care that vexes me in my daily life. Bring me closer to Thee and let me nestle in Thy bosom of love.

Give grace to us all who dwell in this Christian home to bring our troubles and our needs, our joys and our sorrows, to Thee, trusting in Thy help and believing that Thou wilt answer our petitions as we cry unto Thee.

Grant us grace to glorify Thy name. Let not sins that dishonor Thee come into our lives, but let our going out and our coming in, our communications and conversations, hallow Thy name in the community in which we live. I ask all this because of Jesus Christ, our Savior and Friend. Amen.

Effectual Prayer

The effectual, fervent prayer of a righteous man availeth much.
Jas. 5, 16.

Saying prayers is not always praying. A prayer must come from the heart. Lip-worship accomplishes nothing. Therefore James declares by inspiration: "The effectual, fervent prayer of a righteous man availeth much." The prayers of the righteous have accomplished great things. Elijah prayed earnestly that it might not rain in Israel. And it rained not on the earth for three years and six months. Then when Israel acknowledged that the Lord is God, Elijah prayed again, and the heavens gave rain, and the earth brought forth her fruit.

If prayer, however, is to bring to pass such mighty works, then it must be fervent. Such prayer needs earnest preparation. Therefore Jesus says: "Thou, when thou prayest, enter into thy closet, and when thou hast shut thy door, pray to thy Father which is in secret," Matt. 6, 6. Seclude yourself from the world. Close out the thousand

and one thoughts that want to distract your mind. Meditate upon God and His great love in Christ Jesus. If you do, your prayer will be fervent.

Fervent prayer means persistent prayer. Jesus encourages us to such prayer by saying: Ask, and if there be no results, seek, and if there be no answer, knock. We cannot pray persistently unless we are fervent, ardent, and convinced that prayer availeth much.

Fervent prayer implies that we ask for something definite. Generalities often mean nothing. Be specific by asking for this or that blessing at one time. Do not ask for forgiveness in a sweeping, indefinite way, but search the heart and ask God to blot out this and that sin of which you are conscious. That does not mean that we should ignore those sins which we do not know, but it does mean that we should not be indifferent about the things that we have done and said throughout the day. And as some sins stand out boldly at the evening hour, ask God to forgive these and then also those which you do not know.

Fervent prayer implies humility. Pride closes the door to the throne-room of God. Pride makes us think that we have done nothing wrong. Pride makes us self-satisfied. Only he who recognizes the sinfulness of his life will humbly and fervently plead: "God be merciful to me, a sinner."

Fervent prayer makes us patient. In the days of sickness and affliction we often become impatient and irritable. We murmur if God does not answer our prayer at once. Some even secretly rebel. Such attitude makes our prayer-life ineffective.

Fervent prayer means that we confidently believe in the power of prayer. We Christians know that prayer accomplishes much. Many say that answered prayer is fiction. Others say that answered prayer is merely a fancy of a pious imagination.   But we Christians know it to be a fact that God answers prayer. Therefore let us fervently, earnestly, and diligently seek God in prayer through our Lord Jesus Christ.

Prayer

O Thou who hearest prayer, to Thee I come, imploring Thy divine help. I ask Thee that Thou wouldst forgive all my sins of this day and remember them no more. Thou knowest that my lips have not always been clean, that my thoughts have not always been pure, and that my hands have not always served Thee. But today, O Lord, clothe me in the righteousness of Jesus and accept me for His sake and help me in my distress. Relieve me of my suffering and let Thy healing hand rest upon me. Let me know, gracious Father, that Thou art not indifferent to my needs, but art ever eager to bless, to preserve, and to restore both my body and my soul to perfect health. Let me never doubt Thy promises and give me patience and grace to wait upon Thee day after day. I ask all this because of Him who has endured still greater pain on the cross to redeem me that I might be His own, Christ Jesus, my Lord. Amen.

The Power of Prayer

Therefore I say unto you, What things soever ye desire when ye pray, believe that ye receive them, and ye shall have them.
                                        Mark 11, 24.

The power of prayer is often underestimated. We limit the answers to our prayer by our unbelief. "What things soever ye desire, . . . ye shall have them," is the promise of Jesus, and His promises are always true. However, the promise is conditional. We must believe. "When ye pray, believe that ye receive them."

Jesus recognizes the fact that we have needs and desires. God has created us with a desire for food, for companionship, for health. We need shelter and clothing against the winds and the storms and the cold. Above all we need forgiveness, reconciliation with God, peace of heart and mind, strengthening of our faith, patience amid our trials. Jesus knows that we are in need of these things. Therefore He tells us to pray, to make known to God all our wants.

Making known our wants to God with a doubting mind makes our prayer valueless. Merely to say a prayer is useless. This we are doing if we pray without believing.

What are we to believe? "That ye receive them." Our faith should not permit us to question for a moment God's ability and readiness to give according to His will to our welfare, for time and for eternity.

That does not necessarily mean that we shall immediately see the things accomplished for which we ask. If you send a telegram to a brother or sister living five hundred or six hundred miles away from the place you live, asking them to come to you, you do not see them the next moment after you have sent the wire. You do not send some one to the station to meet every train that comes in. In fact, you will not go near the station for hours. But all the while the train is coming at the rate of forty or fifty miles an hour. On it is that brother or sister answering your call. But you do not see them. So God sets things a-moving, thus answering your prayer. That we should believe, and then we shall receive.

But why should we have such faith? Because Jesus Christ gives us this assurance. He, the eternal God, has guaranteed to us that "what things soever ye desire when ye pray, believe that ye receive them, and ye shall have them." What more can we ask? Therefore let us approach the throne of God with a believing heart, make known all our wants and all our needs in the days of health as well as in the days of sickness, confidently believing that He will grant our requests according to His good and gracious will.

Prayer

Lord, Thou art acquainted with all my needs. Nothing is hidden from Thee. Thou hast asked me to come to Thee in prayer, to make known unto Thee all my wants of body and soul. Thou knowest that I need forgiveness. Therefore blot out all my sins through the blood of Jesus Christ. Thou knowest that I need strength to resist the assaults of Satan, who wants to fill me with doubt about Thy mercy. Give me strength to resist and trust unfailingly in Thee. Thou knowest that we need daily food in this home. Bless Thou the labors of the hands that go out to toil today that we all may have those things which we need for the support and wants of the body. Thou knowest that we need peace. Bless our home day after day with Thine everlasting peace that we may be reconciled daily unto Thee and live in harmony and love with one another. In the Savior's name I ask it. Amen.

God Answers Prayer

There hath not failed one word of all His good promise which He promised by the hand of Moses, His servant. — *1 Kings 8, 56.*

God has made surprisingly big promises to those who pray. "Call upon Me in the day of trouble; I will deliver thee," Ps. 50, 15. "Ask, and it shall be given you; seek, and ye shall find; knock, and it shall be opened unto you. For every one that asketh, receiveth; and he that seeketh, findeth; and to him that knocketh it shall be opened," Matt. 7, 7. 8. "He shall call upon Me, and I will answer him; I will be with him in trouble," Ps. 91, 15.

What astonishing promises! Certainly we ought to be found at the throne of God every hour of the day, making known our wants and our needs. But, alas, how seldom we pray!

As we go to the throne-room to make our requests known, we remember that we have not always heeded the call to prayer, that we often have forgotten the Lord in the day of prosperity and health. So prayer reveals us to ourselves. As we ask for favors, we realize that we have not always served the Lord, who is rich in mercy toward us. Therefore we must first seek His forgiveness as we come in prayer, pleading that He would blot out our transgressions through Christ's precious blood.

As we come to God in prayer, pouring out our hearts to Him, we learn that God is very near to every one that seeks Him. He does answer prayer. He does deliver us. This removes every fear from our hearts. This closeness of God lifts us out of despair. I must trust Him, I cannot worry.

Thus as I leave the throne-room with my answered prayers, I come forth from His presence completely transformed. I am hopeful, I believe. I am persuaded that nothing in life or in death today or tomorrow can harm me. Though I may not understand God's methods for today, I know that His thoughts are thoughts of goodness and of mercy toward me. So I will praise the Lord as I patiently wait upon Him.

Thus let us all daily come with our troubles, with our weaknesses, with our sins, to the Lord, believing that every one who asketh, receiveth.

> Oh, what peace we often forfeit,
> Oh, what needless pain we bear,
> All because we do not carry
> Everything to God in prayer!

Prayer

The burdens of life are heavy upon me, O Lord. They want to crush me. I know not whither to turn nor what to do. I am helpless. But Thou hast promised to be very near to those who are in trouble. Therefore I take refuge in Thee, knowing that Thy promises are everlastingly true. My sins sorely vex me; forgive them all through Christ Jesus. The worries of the day want to crush me; lift them from my shoulders, O Lord. My pain greatly distresses me; ease Thou my suffering.

Come Thou into our home and bless it with Thy presence every hour of the day. Fill us all with joy and contentment and peace. Keep us close to Thee and grant that we may ever be united with Thy Christian Church and at last enter into the glories of Thy triumphant people to praise and glorify the Lamb that was slain and has washed us white in His blood. Amen.

Worth Knowing

And we know that all things work together for good to them that love God. — *Rom. 8, 28*.

The days that are before us are hidden from our view. We know not what tomorrow holds and will bring with it. But the Lord promises: "All things work together for good to them that love God." That is worth knowing.

All things — the big things of life that shake us to the very marrow in our bones. Seemingly these big things want to crush us. No misfortune is so dreadful, however, that God cannot turn it to our good.

Not only the big things, but also the insignificant things God turns to our good. The little things of life often irritate and distress us. Often we make mountains out of these trivial matters and rob ourselves of every blessedness of life. If we know this promise of God to be true, that He turns everything to our good, then we will not permit anything to send us into the slough of despair, but we will rather patiently wait upon the Lord.

All things, the big and the insignificant, work together for our good, not measured by today only, but by eternity. When God turns all things to our good, He is not merely considering our physical well-being and present comforts, but above all He has in mind the salvation of our souls. Therefore He takes from us at times that which we most want because He sees that we are beginning to love it more than we love Him. Automobiles, parties, dinners, golf, business, may make us forget God. Therefore God shuts us in and puts us upon our backs that we may realize that man profits nothing if he gains the whole world and loses his own soul.

As we pass through the trials of life, let us hold fast to the promise of God that all things work together for good to them that love Him. Then we shall be hopeful and confident.

Prayer

Gracious Father, my help cometh from Thee. I cannot go through the day safely unless Thou dost take me by the hand. My footsteps falter, and my vision is dim. Today I lean upon Thee, trusting that Thou wilt lead me safely in the paths of righteousness and to eternal life. Many things I cannot understand, O Lord, but I do know that Thou dost love me, for Thou hast given Thy Son Jesus Christ into death that I might live. Remove from my heart every doubt. Give me faith to believe that Thy promises are ever true. Thy ways are not my ways, O Lord, but I know that Thy ways are ways of mercy and grace for those that love Thee.

Wherever I have become impatient with Thee, O Lord, and murmured against Thee, forgive for Jesus' sake and lead me more closely to Thyself. I ask this in Jesus' name. Amen.

The Most Blessed People in the World

O Lord of hosts, blessed is the man that trusteth in Thee.
Ps. 84, 12.

The Christians are the most blessed people in the world. They have a peacefulness of heart and mind that no one else can find. This blessedness is theirs even in the days of sickness. We are told that the Atlantic Ocean, three hundred feet beneath the surface, is perfectly calm. A tremendous storm may be whipping the surface, sweeping the waves across the biggest vessels that plow through the sea, yet a few hundred feet beneath there is not a ripple,

That is a picture of a Christian's life. In this world he may have great trials and vexing difficulties, he may have mighty battles to fight and trying problems to face, yet deep down in his heart there is a perfect calm and peace, which make him the most blessed person in the world.

The Christian is the most blessed person in the world because his heavenly Father is with him. So we are told in John 14, 23: "If a man love Me, he will keep My words; and My Father will love him, and We will come unto him and make Our abode with him." If the Father abides with us, then we need not fear anything. All is well; for if God is with us, who can be against us?

Again, the Christian is the most blessed person in the world because he has the comfort of the Holy Spirit, who brings to his remembrance the precious promises of Scripture. We read in John 14, 26: "But the Comforter, which is the Holy Ghost, whom the Father will send in My name, He shall teach you all things and bring all things to your remembrance, whatsoever I have said unto you." That is why every one of us makes this experience that a Scripture statement or a hymn verse will suddenly come to our mind to comfort us. Ofttimes when we are in church, it seems as though the sermon were being preached only to us. That is the working of the Holy Spirit. If we believe the promises that come to our remembrance through the power of the Spirit of God, we shall find peace of heart and mind.

Once more, the Christian is the most blessed person in the world because he is reconciled with God. This assurance we find in John 14, 27: "Peace I leave with you, My peace I give unto you; not as the world giveth, give I unto you. Let not your heart be troubled, neither let it be afraid." This peace of God has been purchased by Christ with His holy, precious blood. Through this holy, innocent blood of Jesus every sin is blotted out, and God remembers it no more. There is nothing now that can condemn the believer. Knowing this brings us this wonderful blessedness.

Therefore in the day of trouble and in the hour of trial, as we face the critical moments of life, let us cling to these wonderful promises, which quiet the heart and fill us with safety even amid the storms of life and give us that blessedness which is found only in the hearts of the people of God.

Prayer

Jesus, blessed Redeemer, fill me with the blessedness of a Christian's happy life. I look for Thy presence, for it sweetens my life and purifies my thoughts. Come as the Lover of my soul and cleanse me from sin and clothe me in the robe of Thy righteousness. Send thy Holy Spirit to bring to my remembrance that Thou hast purchased me with Thy precious blood.

Wonderful Savior, Thou knowest that great dangers beset me. Preserve me in body and soul as I pass through this crisis and lead me and keep me unto that Great Day when I shall behold Thee face to face to rejoice in Thy presence eternally. 'Lord, others entice me and seek to lure me away from Thee. Let me see the deceitfulness of their ways and watch against their cunning. Speak to me again and again through Thy precious Word and assure me of Thy undying love. Keep us all who dwell in this home faithful and true unto Thee, even as Thou hast been faithful and true unto us. I ask this because Thou art our Lord and our Redeemer. Amen.

"Why Has This Befallen Me?"

And Gideon said unto Him, O my Lord, if the Lord be with us, why, then, is all this befallen us? — *Judg. 6, 13.*

The story is this: The children of Israel did evil in the sight of the Lord. Therefore God delivered them into the hands of the people of Midian, who again and again invaded the country at the time of the harvest. Throughout the summer the Israelites would work their fields and in the fall gather in their crops. As soon as they had harvested their grain, the Midianites would invade the country and take possession of everything. Though the land brought forth abundantly Israel did not enjoy the fruits thereof.

At this time Gideon lived in Israel. One day he was secretly threshing his wheat, hiding from the Midianites. While he was threshing, the Angel of the Lord appeared to him. It was then that Gideon put this question: "If the Lord be with us, why, then, is all this befallen us?"

We ask this same question time and again. It is natural that we should ask it, for God has promised otherwise. He has said: "I will never leave thee nor forsake thee."

Then, God has done otherwise in the past. He has given us health, food, clothing, and shelter. He has opened His hand and satisfied our wants and needs. Therefore we Christian people likewise ask: If, after all, we are God's people, why, then, do these things befall us? Why do we have a harder time in making a living than the ungodly? Why have we so much sickness? Why are we not as prosperous as others?

It is reasonable to expect an answer. And God gives us an answer.

In regard to Israel, God says that they have not met the conditions which He made. They were to serve Him, and they were serving other gods and forgetting Him. This was offensive to the Lord. They had broken their agreement with Him. Therefore God was chastening or correcting them.

In regard to you and me God's answer is likewise found in the Scriptures. We ask, "Why, then, is all this befallen us?" and God answers in Heb. 12, 6: "Whom the Lord loveth He chasteneth."

To chasten means to correct. Parents who love their

children correct them. The very fact that they correct their children proves that they are interested in their welfare. Mothers correct their boys and girls because they want them to grow up as Christian gentlemen and gentlewomen. God corrects us that we might grow up as Christian men and Christian women and partakers of the glories of heaven. God tells us that whatever befalls us is coming to pass for the sole purpose of leading us to heaven. Even the goodness the Lord shows the wicked is not without purpose. Therefore we are told in Romans 2, 4: "Or despisest thou the riches of His goodness and forbearance and long-suffering, not knowing that the goodness of God leadeth thee to repentance?"

Some things befall us in life to jolt us out of our self-complacency. Many of us are very much satisfied with themselves. We are overcome by a spiritual drowsiness. Often you have heard that drivers become drowsy at the wheel. That is dangerous. Sometimes a little jolt will arouse them completely, and they escape an accident. So in life we often go on self-satisfied, and God jolts us out of this indifference by sending troubles and difficulties. These things have a sobering effect upon us.

Trials and troubles also befall us to purify our souls. On sultry days a storm will clear the atmosphere. How much better the air we breathe after the storm has passed over! So God, through trials and tribulations, develops faith and a Christian character. We have a clearer vision of God. We seek Him with greater zeal. We learn that, after all, God answers our prayers and turns everything to our good. So we learn to love Him more than the things of this world.

If, then, things befall us in life that want to make us doubt the loving-kindness of God, let us search our own hearts and review our yesterdays to see whether our drowsiness or indifference, our sin or our coldness, is not the reason why God's correcting hand is laid upon us. Such self-searching will draw us nearer to God and save our souls.

Prayer

Gracious Father, Thou hast loved also me with an everlasting love and given me the blessed assurance that, even though I look through a glass, darkly, Thy ways are ever ways of love and mercy, that Thou art seeking to bless me. With Thy gracious hand uphold me and let Thy strength be my strength.

We are Thy people, who by Thy marvelous grace have come to know Jesus Christ as our Lord and Savior and believe in Him. Keep us in this faith, which justifies us in Thy sight. Bless us daily with Thy divine forgiveness and grant us grace to walk with Thee every hour of the day that Thy name may be glorified by the lives that we live. Fill us with peace of heart and mind and ever keep us united with Thy Christian Church. Grant that nothing be dearer to us than Thy Word, which is "a power of God unto salvation to every one that believeth." I ask this in the name of Him who has become poor that I might be rich for all eternity, Christ Jesus, our Savior. Amen.

The Cure for Depression

Why art thou cast down, O my soul, and why art thou disquieted in me? Hope thou in God; for I shall yet praise Him for the help of His countenance. — *Ps. 42, 5.*

Here we have the cure for depression: "Hope thou in God." Most human beings must fight the so-called blues time and again. In days of sickness and affliction hearts are heavy, and often the light is gone out of the eyes.

The Christian's skies are never all gloom. The Christian knows that there must be light somewhere wherever there are shadows. Behind every shadow and behind every cloud which darkens His day there is a loving Father, who never slumbers or sleeps. This enables the Christian to go on amid his troubles and sicknesses and afflictions, certain that his heavenly Father is with him and gives him sufficient strength for the day and for the ordeal.

In life, joys and sorrows counterbalance one another. Therefore the Christian looks forward hopefully and courageously in the days of trouble. To reach the heights of faith and blessedness and peace amid the troubles of life is often a hard climb. But if we cling to the promises of God, we shall yet praise Him for the help which He has given us in the days of adversity. Therefore our souls should not be cast down. We Christians have no right to be depressed and blue.

Yet often we are greatly disquieted. "Why art thou cast down, O my soul?" The soul is often cast down because everything seems to be going wrong. There are many disappointments, much suffering, torturous nights, restless days, and financial worries. Amid all these God seems to be silent. The heavens are like brass. Seemingly God does not answer our prayers.

"And why art thou disquieted within me?" Our soul is disquieted by our sins. We know that we have done contrary to the divine will of God. Often we have omitted to give God first place in our lives. We have passed by on the other side as we travel down to Jericho. But "to him that knoweth to do good and doeth it not, to him it is sin," Jas. 4, 17. In the day of trouble we become more fully aware of the sinfulness of our hearts. This troubles us. Above all we are disquieted with doubts. We doubt God's goodness and justice. Our distressed hearts feel that God is not treating us as He should. He lets us suffer while the ungodly prosper.

There is but one remedy for this depression of the soul: "Hope thou in God!"

How do we hope in God? We must take Him by His word, cling to Him, believe His promises, trust in His help. God is not indifferent to our prayers, but does answer them. He is not insensible to our plea for mercy. He abundantly pardons through Christ. He is not unconcerned about our doubts. He will show us that He thinks of us and that His thoughts are thoughts of mercy. Therefore "hope thou in God."

Every one that hopes in God will yet praise Him because He has answered his prayers, forgiven his sins, brought peace to his heart, and given strength and help in his weakness and distress.

Prayer

Heavenly Father, Thou hast promised to be my Refuge and my Strength in the days of trouble. Thou knowest how heavily the burden of this affliction is resting upon me. Therefore I come to Thee as the one Rock to which I can cling, the one Refuge in which there is sure hiding. Let Thy goodness rest upon me. Forgive me all my transgressions. Remove from me every doubt which questions Thy power to help and Thy willingness to save. Let Satan not lead me into despair. O Lord, Thou art my Shepherd; lead me. Thou art my Pilot; uphold me amid the troubled waters and lead me at last safely to the haven of eternal peace. I plead with Thee for the Redeemer's sake. Amen.

The Peace past Understanding

Peace I leave with you, My peace I give unto you; not as the world giveth, give I unto you. Let not your heart be troubled, neither let it be afraid. — *John 14, 27.*

This wonderful promise Jesus gives you as you pass through the troubled waters of life. No one can give you a more blessed assurance of peace than Jesus Christ. If you believe these words of our Lord, — and why should you not? — then you can look hopefully into the tomorrow.

The human heart has three outstanding needs: We need peace against the accusations of conscience; we need a haven of safety in the day of trouble; and we need hope when face to face with death and eternity.

Jesus gives peace to the conscience. Sin robs us of peace. Jesus takes all our sins and iniquities upon Himself, goes with them to the cross, and there makes complete atonement with His holy, precious blood. He stands in our place, taking the blame and the consequence. The justice of God demands that sin be punished, and in Jesus this justice of God has been satisfied. The sinner who believes goes out free, robed in the righteousness of Christ. That assures him of acquittal against every accusation.

Christ offers us a haven of safety in the day of trouble. We need not face the storms alone. We can go to Him in prayer, and as we come to Him, He guides us with a steady hand and leads us safely into the haven. As Christians we are never alone, not even in the day of trouble. At the beginning of the day we often may feel as though we could not live through another twenty-four hours, as though the troubles would completely crush us; but when the evening comes, we discover that Christ has given us sufficient strength. This we learn day after day. Therefore we feel secure even though we pass through the troubled waters.

Jesus fills us with hope in the hour of death. Being reconciled with God, we know that heaven is our home. Not for a moment has Jesus ever left us in doubt about heaven. "In My Father's house are many mansions; if it were not so, I would have told you. I go to prepare a place for you. And if I go and prepare a place for you, I will come again and receive you unto Myself that where I am, there ye may be also," John 14, 2. 3. When every earthly hope fails, this glorious promise becomes more real, and we look forward to that home where God shall wipe away all tears from our eyes and heal all our heartaches.

With such a promise and with faith in this promise we cannot become discouraged or disheartened, but must go on filled with cheerfulness, hope, and patience.

Prayer

I need Thee every hour, gracious Lord, to uphold me amid the troubled waters of life lest I go down amid the worry and care, the hopelessness and despair, that besets me. Lord, I am in sore straits and know not whither to turn, but Thou hast promised never to forsake me. Be Thou my Stay and Strength today. Forgive me my sins and transgressions. Remember them no more, but blot them out through the blood of Jesus Christ. I place myself, my body and my soul, in Thy gracious hands. Fill me with the blessed assurance that in Thee there is forgiveness and help, strength and safety, today, tomorrow, and forevermore. In Jesus' name I ask it. Amen.

The Gospel of the Greater Love

Greater love hath no man than this, that a man lay down his life for his friends. — *John 15, 13.*

The greatest demonstration of the love of God is found in Christ Jesus. Christ laid down His life, not only for His friends, but even for the ungodly; for He died for us while we were yet sinners. He laid down His life voluntarily. Therefore the death of Jesus Christ was not a slaughter, but a sacrifice of love. He willed to give His life. He deliberately chose to suffer upon the cross. He knew that this was the only way in which He could redeem the human race from sin and death.

To achieve His work, Christ gave His life. He fulfilled His mission by dying, by dying the very death He did die, despised and rejected of men, numbered among the transgressors. He went down into outer darkness, where there is weeping and gnashing of teeth, until the bitter cry came forth from His parched lips, "My God, My God, why hast Thou forsaken Me?" He could not go into a deeper depth, for there is only one place where God could completely forsake Him, in hell.

Christ gave His life-blood. With this blood-sacrifice

He made atonement. His death was a substitutionary death. The wages of sin is death, and the Lord laid upon Him the iniquity of us all, and Jesus paid for it. Therefore Jesus was more than an exemplar. He was not only a way-shower. He was not merely a sign-post that was to point the way that we should go. No, He was the Way itself, the Savior, who by the shedding of His blood made full payment for the sins of man in the just courts of God the Father. Truly, there is no greater love than this.

We Christian people therefore come to the Cross for salvation. We find here forgiveness and peace. For this reason this Gospel of greater love is a source of constant joy to us. Through Christ's atonement we are reconciled to God and are heirs of life eternal.

Since this "greater love" has saved us without any merit or worthiness on our part, we believers are always moved in gratitude to live for Christ and to serve Him. We cannot return to our former service of sin. We cannot do otherwise than love Him who first loved us. Our whole life shall be dedicated and consecrated to Christ. This our Christian life is an expression of appreciation on our part, who were called out of darkness into the Kingdom, redeemed and saved.

And as we ponder upon all that Jesus has done, the giving of His life that we might live eternally, we will patiently and cheerfully bear the burdens of the day and the trials of life.

Prayer

Lord Jesus, Thou spotless Lamb of God, Thou hast loved me with a love so great and so wonderful that Thou hast given Thy life to make me Thine own. Grant that I may ever remember that through Thee only I have peace, and hope, and salvation. In the midst of my trials and sufferings and afflictions bring to my mind that Thou hast suffered still greater pain on Calvary that I might not suffer eternally.

Grant that each and every one who dwells within this home may be saved by this faith in Thee and daily and richly find forgiveness of all sins. Let our daily conversation, hallow Thy name and glorify Thee in the community in which we live that all may know that Thou dost abide and dwell in our midst day after day. Amen.

The Restored Soul

The Lord is my Shepherd. . . . He restoreth my soul.
Ps. 23, 1. 3.

God created man in His own image in the beginning of time. We ought, then, to be perfect in our holiness and blameless in our righteousness and without a mar or blemish on our physical body. Mankind, however, is far from perfect today. Our bodies become sick, they suffer pain and distress, and they die. Our souls become blackened with sin, our conscience is seared with guilt, our mind is filled with doubt, despair, and worry, and our life with discontent.

What has robbed us of the perfection in which God created us? Sin has entered into the world, and in its trail followed the ills and the woes of life. Sin has marred our body, dulled our conscience, poisoned our mind, and besmirched our soul.

Sin spells death. "The wages of sin is death." "The soul that sinneth, it shall die." So God decrees in His holy and just Law.

But God has also a good and gracious will toward man and therefore in His great love sent His Son, Jesus Christ, into the world that He, in our place and for us, might take upon Himself the iniquity of us all and pay the penalty for our sins. Thus He restores our soul.

Through Christ's precious blood we are cleansed, and we are cleansed from every sin. "Forasmuch as ye know that ye were not redeemed with corruptible things, as silver and gold, from your vain conversation received by tradition from your fathers, but with the precious blood of Christ, as of a Lamb without blemish and without spot." Daily we Christians know "that the blood of Jesus Christ, His Son, cleanseth us from all sin." Thus the soul is restored day by day.

This is of special comfort to us in times of sickness. When we are shut in by suffering, pain, and affliction, we feel the burden of sin in greater measure than before. Sin becomes more real to us. Sickness makes the soul sensitive, — and our soul should be sensitive, realizing that every sin, be it in thought, word, or deed, grieves God. By the Gospel of Jesus Christ, however, we are filled with comfort and strength. We can go to this Good Shepherd, who knows all our needs and wants and who loves us. To Him we confess our sin and admit our guilt. As we come, He restores our soul and brings into our hearts and minds that peace which passes all human understanding.

In the days of trials and troubles let us not lose faith, but trustingly turn to the Good Shepherd, for He restores our soul and heals our body.

Prayer

O Thou great Shepherd of my soul, to Thee I come for healing. Heal Thou my body and heal Thou my soul. I can find no peace but in Thee. Thou have promised to be with me when I pass through the swellings of Jordan and to uphold me with Thine almighty hand. Fill me this day with a faith that will never doubt Thee and Thy promises. Restore my soul unto Thy grace. Give me strength to bear patiently and uncomplainingly the trials of the day and keep me steadfast in Thy Word.

Bless each one in this home with this alone-saving faith and cause them all to turn day after day to Thee as the Good Shepherd that through Thee their souls may be cleansed from every sin, restored and made anew, and kept in Thy grace for time and eternity. Amen.

Called by Name

I have called thee by thy name, thou art Mine. — *Is. 43, 1.*

"Life is a chance," many, tell us. To such life is like a roulette-wheel, which stops at random at any number without plan, without purpose, and without reason. Those who believe this deny God. They speak of blind fate and of luck.

Others are not ready to rule God out of existence. Nevertheless they believe that God is too much occupied with the big things of the universe and the history of the world to be concerned about little me.

There is, however, very little consolation in this. If God is so preoccupied, I will be crushed between the big things of life. The Scriptures give us a greater promise and assure us of a more loving comfort. They tell us that God knows each one of us by name. God Himself declares through His Word that He has inscribed our names upon the palms of His hands. We are personally known to God. He knows our mistakes as well as our troubles. He knows our sorrows as well as our joys. God does not treat us like so many in a crowd, but He calls each one by name. He called Adam by name when he had sinned. He called Peter by name when He restored him to discipleship. He called Mary by name when she stood outside of the grave weeping. He calls you and me by name and sympathizes with us in our tears and heartaches, in our problems and worries, in our sicknesses and pains.

What does God say to us as He calls? "Thou art Mine." God claims us as His own. He claims us because He has redeemed us through Christ with His holy, precious blood. The Lord Jesus has paid the price of our salvation. As the redeemed our names are written in the Book of Life.

To hear the call of God, we must know His voice.

God speaks to us through His Word. As we hear the voice of this Word, we shall find Him giving us the heartening assurances that He will be with us and go with us all the way. Let us follow the voice of His Word and let us abide in His presence. Then we shall discover that no battle is fought alone and no burden is crushing us.

Prayer

Heavenly Father, Thou hast called me out of darkness into Thy presence and hast become my Refuge day after day. Thou hast upheld me in my troubles and hast shielded me against sin and doubt. Thou hast promised to be with me in the day of trouble and hast never forsaken me. As I come, I am mindful of my own sins. I am unworthy of Thy many blessings. But nevertheless I come because Thou hast invited all the weary and heavy-laden to come unto Thee through Thy Son Jesus Christ. In Thy great mercy cleanse me from all sin. Accept me as Thine own through Him who has loved me unto death.

Fill each one in this home with this peace and joy of forgiveness. Bless the labors of our hands. Give us cheerful hearts and care-free minds. Keep us faithful to Thy alone-saving Word. I ask this for the sake of Him who has loved me unto death, Christ Jesus, my Lord. Amen.

Christ's Clinic

And Jesus went forth and saw a great multitude and was moved with compassion toward them; and He healed their sick.
Matt. 14, 14.

Jesus acknowledges the existence of pain. He does not merely recognize that man suffers and then lets it go at that, but He sympathizes with us in our troubles and is deeply concerned about our sorrows. Therefore the Scriptures again and again tell us that Jesus was moved with compassion as He looked upon the ailing multitude and the suffering sick.

Jesus knew what causes these ills of life. To the man

sick of the palsy He said: "Thy sins be forgiven thee." Sin has brought all the woes and sorrows and sufferings into this world. To the impenitent sickness comes to curb them in their sinful pursuits and to call them to repentance. To the believers troubles come to chasten them and to win them away from the world. Sickness also comes in the lives of Christian people to make them more sympathetic with those who are in trouble.

Christ is not indifferent to our pain. He promises to help us. He either lifts the burden from us or gives us the strength to bear it. He fills us with patience and gives us a contented heart. Above all He promises that we shall be delivered completely from all consequences of sin in the world to come; for in heaven there shall be "no more pain."

Jesus directs us to prayer in the day of trouble. Therefore we should seek every hour the throne of God. The Lord will never turn from us; for Jesus is just as compassionate today as He was in the days of His sojourn here upon earth. Even though it seems as though our prayers are unanswered, nevertheless we can be certain that, if we continue praying, we shall receive help. Sometimes the Lord delays help to make us more fervent, more earnest, and more determined in prayer.

Prayer

I humbly bow down, Lord Jesus, to receive Thy benediction and blessing in this very hour of suffering and pain. I need Thee to keep me content and satisfied. I need Thee to help me overcome the assaults of Satan, who wants me to doubt the power of Thy grace. Be Thou very near to me when these thoughts assail me.

Shine Thou into my heart with Thy love and mercy and forgive all my sins. Let me find real joy in Thee and fill me with a spirit of thoughtfulness and love.

Let not the cares of the world and the deceitfulness of riches burden my heart. Let us all remember that Thy mercies are new every morning. Bless each one who must face the task of earning his daily bread. Provide us with food day by day and give manna from heaven to sustain our souls. Dwell in our home and in our hearts. We ask this of Thee, who art the Bread of Life come from heaven. Amen.

He Thinketh upon Me

How precious also are Thy thoughts unto me, O God! How great is the sum of them! — *Ps. 139, 17.*

Truly it is comforting to know that God thinks upon us. What are God's thoughts toward us? His thoughts are thoughts of love. That is why He gave His only-begotten Son that whosoever believeth on Him should not perish, but have everlasting life. God's thoughts are thoughts of peace. That is why we have redemption through the blood of Jesus Christ, who has atoned for all our sins and reconciled us with our heavenly Father. God's thoughts are thoughts of forgiveness. Therefore He stretches out His hands of mercy day after day and invites us to come. Summing up these thoughts of love, peace, and forgiveness, we have salvation.

These precious thoughts of God are toward us. God is concerned about each individual soul. He calls each one by name. He knows the wants of each and every one of us. He is acquainted with my problems and with your pains.

God's thoughts are toward each family. As one by one they go out in the morning to perform their daily tasks, we know that God protects them. Therefore we willingly place them into His hands. We ask Him to guide, direct, and lead them through the day.

God's thoughts are toward the Church. That is why the Cross of Christ has towered over the wrecks of time. Sometimes we feel as though the Church were losing ground, as though the battle were lost and the Gospel defeated. But God never forgets His Church. It shall endure throughout the ages, and the Gospel shall reach the ends of the earth to proclaim peace and hope to the sin-troubled world.

God's thoughts are toward the nations. He protects our country against the foes from within and without. He blesses the nation with men of judgment and wisdom. He decks the fields with abundance. He gives prosperity to the people.

God is with us in the day of sickness. His thoughts are ever seeking our good, even in the days of chastening. Even though we cannot understand His ways and think that He has forgotten us, nevertheless we shall learn in the end to praise Him because His thoughts were thoughts of mercy and of goodness toward us all.

Prayer

Praise be to Thee, O God of life and salvation, because of Thy tender thoughts and loving-kindness toward me. In Thee do I find strength and help. In my loneliness I have found comfort in knowing that Thou art thinking upon me and therefore art weaving all things for my good, not only for today, but throughout the length of days and eternity. Forgive every unkind thought that has come into my heart, every murmuring complaint that I have made against Thee. Let me know in the daytime that Thy thoughts are toward me, and in the night that Thou dost not slumber nor sleep.

Bless Thou our home and make it a forecourt of the eternal home. Bless Thou our nation and let righteousness prevail. Bless Thou our Church and preserve in it the Gospel in its purity and bring many to this perfect peace in Thee.

Uphold me with Thy hand in these my afflictions and let me ever know that the glories that await me are eternal. Therefore into Thy hands I place myself and all my loved ones for Jesus' sake. Amen.

The Overrunning Cup

My cup runneth over. — *Ps. 23, 5.*

The Christian always finds something in life for which he can praise God. He is always counting His blessings. Like David he finds that his cup is running over with the goodness of the Lord. If David had reason to praise the Lord, then we, too, can sing unto Him who has been our Keeper and our Light and our Salvation. David had many times passed through the valley of sorrow and trouble. Persecuted, he was in want; exiled, he lived in the mountains; envied, many attempts were made upon his life. Yea, he even had to flee from his own son, who had stolen the hearts of the people and had risen in rebellion against him. Yet he exclaims in this Psalm of psalms: "My cup runneth over."

Our cup runneth over with natural blessings. God gives us bread day after day. He shelters us against the cold and the heat, the wind and the sleet. Our homes are not mere hovels; our beds are not stone slabs; our food is dainty and tasty. God is daily providing us with the things that we need for the support and want of the body.

Our cup is running over with personal blessings. We are surrounded by loved ones who are deeply concerned about our well-being and comfort. We have hosts of friends, who ever seek to gladden our lonely hours. We are privileged to belong to the Christian Church, and the prayers of our fellow-believers ascend to the throne of God for us.

Our cup is running over with spiritual blessings. God has given us His Word in its truth and purity and His Sacraments as a token of His love. Through these He brings to us forgiveness and peace. We have the privilege of prayer, and we have had the blessed experience of answered prayer. Therefore even in the days of sickness and affliction we can say with David that God has prepared for us a table which is rich in blessings and that the cup is running over with the goodness of the Lord.

Prayer

Thou hast been wonderfully good to me, O Lord, for Thou hast blessed me day after day and given me strength to face the trials of this affliction. Thou hast made my days hopeful and the nights restful. I am not worthy of this Thy goodness and mercy, for I am sinful indeed. Yet Thou thinkest upon me and forgivest all mine iniquity.

Make me mindful of Thy goodness and fill my heart with praise at morning, noon, and night. Let not the cares of life crowd out of my thoughts the one thing needful. As the cup of Thy mercy runneth over, accept this my hymn of praise and my song of appreciation for the sake of Jesus Christ, my Lord. Amen.

We Walk Together, My Lord and I

As ye have therefore received Christ Jesus the Lord, so walk ye in Him. — *Col. 2, 6.*

There is only one religion in the world that can bring us into the right relationship with God — the religion of the Bible. In the Bible, God speaks to us. He tells us that sin has come between Him and us and that this sin must be removed if we are to be saved. But just here lies the difficulty. We cannot remove sin. That power lies not within us, for we are spiritually dead. Therefore God tells us that He has sent His Son Jesus Christ into the world that by the shedding of His blood He might remove from us the guilt of sin. By Jesus Christ salvation has been completed.

Through faith in Jesus Christ we are personally cleansed from every sin. Therefore Jesus Christ alone can reconcile us to His Father and bring peace into our hearts. Being cleansed, we become temples of the Lord. We receive the Lord Jesus into our hearts.

If we have received Christ as our Savior into our hearts, naturally we love Him, and we walk with Him. But how do we walk with Him?

In the first place, by faithfully abiding in His Word. This Word is the one thing needful.

Then we walk with Christ Jesus in prayer. Prayer keeps us in daily touch with the Lord.

We walk with Jesus by going to Holy Communion. In the Lord's Supper, Jesus Christ gives us with the bread and with the cup His body and His blood for the remission of our sins. Through this Sacrament we become one with Him. "The cup of blessing which we bless, is it not the communion of the blood of Christ? The bread which we break, is it not the communion of the body of Christ? For we, being many, are one bread and one body; for we are all partakers of that one bread," 1 Cor. 10, 16. 17.

Thus God speaks to us through His Word and blesses us through the Sacrament, and we speak to God through prayer.

As we walk with the Lord Jesus Christ, we acknowledge His loving protection and His daily help. Therefore let us trust in Him even though seemingly everything is going wrong.

Prayer

Lord Jesus, merciful Savior, enter Thou into our home and abide with us. Be Thou present at every meal and bless our daily bread. Above all, enter Thou into our hearts and make them temples of Thine. In all our conversation teach us to remember that Thou art listening to every word and art acquainted with our very thoughts. Being mindful of Thy presence, give grace to us all to please Thee.

Forgive us all our sins. I confess that I have not always been faithful to Thee. Thou knowest how weak and helpless I am and how strong and powerful Satan and his angels are. Help me, O Lord, and have mercy upon me. Grant unto us all to put on the whole armor of God that we may quench the fiery darts of Satan. Lord, be not ashamed of us as we have often been ashamed of Thee, but forgive us, bless us, and keep us. Be Thou our Companion and Friend day after day. Amen.

Slaves of Jesus

For I am Thy servant. — *Ps. 143, 12.*

We are slaves of Jesus Christ. He has bought us with His blood and made us His own. All that we have belongs to Him. Since we belong body and soul to Him, He takes care of us. He provides for our daily needs. He restores our soul by daily cleansing it from sin.

As servants we are obedient. We hear His voice and follow Him. In His Word we are told what to do and what not to do. This Word makes known unto us the way to life. As we go through the day, the Lord directs us through this Word unto the paths of righteousness.

This Word reveals to us truths that we could not know otherwise. These revelations permit us to look into eternity, beyond this earthly life with its sorrows and tears. Through faith we understand these truths and find in them comfort and hope. With Samuel of old we therefore declare: "Speak, Lord, for Thy servant heareth."

As servants Christ takes care of us. He provides us with those things that we need for the support and want of the body. He looks after our welfare and our safety. He guides us through the day and is with us in the night-watches. Therefore we can trustingly put ourselves into His everlasting arms, knowing that He will protect us from all evil. He is our loving Master, who has purchased us with His precious blood because He loved us with an everlasting love.

Since we are His own, servants who have been redeemed by His blood, we can go to Him in prayer, telling Him all our needs and seeking His aid every hour of the day. As we do this, we may confidently believe that He will answer our cry and help us in our need.

Prayer

I lift up mine eyes unto Thee, O Lord, from whence cometh my help. Thou art my Keeper, whose loving care watches over me by day and by night. In Thee only can I find safety. In the secret of Thy tabernacle I can find peace. My sin is ever before me, but I know that Thy loving-kindness and tender mercy will make me whiter than snow. Fill me with an undying appreciation of this Thy love in Christ Jesus.

Bring this message of peace unto all who are troubled and distressed. Bless Thy Church as it goes forth with this message. Grant that, wherever the glad news of reconciliation is told, hearts will be ready to receive it. Let not the noise and the din and the glitter and glamor of life keep this blessed peace out of the hearts of Thy people who dwell within these walls. We ask this in the name of Him who died that we might live, Christ Jesus, our Lord. Amen.

Called Saints

Among whom are ye also the called of Jesus Christ, . . . beloved of God, called to be saints. — *Rom. 1, 6. 7.*

Paul tells us here that we are called to be saints. Note well that we are called. It lies not within our power to make ourselves saints. Jesus Christ by His death on the cross has redeemed us, and by the Holy Spirit faith has been created in us in this Jesus as our Lord and Savior, and thus we have been made saints of God. As the potter, finding a defect in his vessel, remakes it, so we have been recreated by the Holy Spirit.

As we are remade, we are cleansed and purged. So we become the beloved of God. God loves us in Christ. It is a wonderful thought to know that God loves us. As God's beloved we are called to be saints.

To be a saint means to live in constant fellowship with God. As Paul states it: "Whether therefore ye eat or drink, or whatsoever ye do, do all to the glory of God," 1 Cor. 10, 31.

Living in fellowship with God means that we pray morning, noon, and night. The Christian is a friend of God, and friends speak to one another often, yea, daily.

Living in fellowship with God means that we read the Scriptures. The Bible is God's love-letter to the human race. What comforting promises, what blessed assurances, what heartening words are not found in the Bible! These have been given to us who are called saints that we might find in them consolation and strength.

As saints of God we patiently wait upon the Lord. God's saints pass through trials and tribulations. But if we are His beloved, He is with us and in sympathy with our needs. Therefore we do not murmur, much less rebel against Him, but receive from His hands the good as well as that which is seemingly evil. Knowing that God promises to take care of us, we lift up our eyes to Him as the Preserver of our bodies and the Keeper of our souls.

The saints of God are filled with a joyous blessedness because they know that God loves them. The saint has found peace; yea, the saint finds daily peace in his Lord; for he knows that the blood of Jesus Christ cleanses and purges him from all sins.

Prayer

All goodness flows from Thee, most gracious Father, and therefore I lift up my heart to Thee. Remember me in Thy tender mercies as the sorrows of life distress me. Often there are battles within and fears without. I am distressed with pain and with grief. But Thou hast promised to keep me, O Lord. I find no other place of refuge but in Thee. Let Thine everlasting arms be around me to protect my soul from doubt and unbelief and my body from pain and distress. Often I have grieved Thee, O Lord; forgive me my sins. Bless this home with Thy loving presence and keep us steadfast and faithful to Thee unto the end. We ask this in the name of the Redeemer, Christ Jesus. Amen.

Incorruptible in Christ

Being born again, not of corruptible seed, but of incorruptible, by the Word of God, which liveth and abideth forever.
1 Pet. 1, 23.

Simon, the son of Jona, one day met Jesus as he, Simon, was pursuing his daily task of fishing. Jesus had before this changed his name to Peter. Thereafter Simon Johnson gave Jesus first place in his life and put everything at Christ's disposal.

Life was different after Simon had met Jesus. This man was now made of different stuff. He was a new creature, an heir to the eternal kingdom of Jesus Christ. Thus he became incorruptible, deathless.

As Christians we, too, are born again, born into the kingdom of Jesus Christ. We therefore belong to Him and are of incorruptible seed. We cannot perish; "neither shall any man pluck them out of My hand," says Jesus.

Everything in this world is perishable. All flesh is as grass, and even the glory of man is as the flower of the grass. We live but a few years in this world. Very few attain the three score and ten years of which the psalmist speaks. All material things are perishable. With one crash fortunes are wiped out. Within one moment death strikes men and women dead. A man starts out in the morning, climbing rapidly to success, and before night he is stricken down by an accident, never to walk again. Even the glory of man is passing. In a hundred years from to-day very few will be known who are living at this hour. Only a few names find their way into the histories of the world.

But the Christian is not of such perishable stuff. His name is written in the Book of Life. He lives forever, all because he belongs to God and is born again of incorruptible seed.

If we belong to God, then our whole life glorifies Him. In sickness and in health, in joyous moments and in critical hours, we will act differently than the people of this world. Our faith will lift us above the ordinary sufferer and make us hopeful and cheerful.

We are born again of an incorruptible seed, by the Word of God. Only the Word can make us new creatures. This Word endureth forever and day after day keeps us in the faith.

This Word, which makes of you new creatures, is preached unto you as a child of God. This glorious message is yours. You are born again, and therefore all sin is blotted out. You are living under grace and therefore are safe for time and eternity.

Prayer

Be Thou my Refuge and my Strength and keep me unspotted from the world as incorruptible seed. Therefore I come to Thee in this hour to consecrate and dedicate myself unto Thee. The world that surrounds me wants to draw me away from Thee, O Lord. Preserve me and keep me. Teach me to watch and pray every moment of the day. Lord, Thou knowest how weak and helpless I am. Be Thou my Strength. Thou knowest how doubt and impatience want to take hold of me; teach me to wait upon Thee. Forgive me all my sins and make me Thine forever, joint heir with Christ in Thy eternal kingdom. For Jesus' sake hear Thou my prayer. Amen.

Passing Safely Through Troubled Waters

When thou passest through the waters, I will be with thee.
Is. 43, 2.

Life holds troubles and sorrows. God tells us to expect this. "We must through much tribulation enter into the kingdom of God," Acts 14, 22. But God promises: "When thou passest through the waters, I will be with thee." That is worth knowing, for we all pass through troubled waters as we journey on to eternity. These troubled waters are sickness, afflictions, unemployment, loss of money, loss of friends, and disappointments. As we pass through these troubled waters, doubts fill the heart, doubts as to the justice of God and the truthfulness of His Word.

When we pass through these troubled waters, God promises to be with us. In our sickness and in our affliction He promises to be our Help. His hand of mercy will heal us. Amid the misfortunes of life, unemployment, loss of money, He tells us that in the end we shall lack nothing, but receive daily and richly sufficient to satisfy all our needs. In the hours when we feel as though we had not a friend in the world, He draws nigh to us as our Companion to cheer us through His Word and to show us that all these things come to pass to carry out His divine will.

This is worth knowing, that, as the heaven is high above the earth, so great is His mercy toward us every day. As He has been with us in our yesterdays, so He will be with us today and in our tomorrows, mercifully removing sin, giving us strength to bear the burdens of the day, and filling us with hope that in the tomorrow all will be well.

Prayer

Heavenly Father, I am out on the uncharted sea of life. The storms are raging, and I am helpless. I come to Thee. Thy Word is a compass guiding me into the narrow path, which leads safely into the haven of eternal peace. Fill me with a love for Thy Word that I may meditate upon it day and night.

I know, O Lord, that I have not always loved Thee with all my heart. I have not always sought Thy Word. I have not always loved Thy Gospel. Forgive me, O Lord. Blot out all these sins and remember them no more. Amid the troubles that beset me today give me a faith that will trust in Thee and in Thy guidance.

Bless our home with Thy divine presence. Guard each one of us from sin and temptation. Shut Thou the door and close us in and protect us from every danger of body and soul. I ask this in the name of our Savior. Amen.

The Victory of the Disheartened Soul

And seek not ye what ye shall eat or what ye shall drink, neither be ye of doubtful mind. — *Luke 12, 29.*

Often as we go along the street or the country lane in the evening hours, we are frightened by shadows, sometimes our own. After we have discovered that it is only a shadow and recovered from our fright, we smile. In life there are many things that want to frighten us and cause us to be filled with worry and anxious thoughts. After all, most of them prove to be shadows.

Jesus understood human nature as none other. Therefore He repeatedly tells us not to be troubled nor anxious, but to trust in God, to believe His promises. Too often we rob ourselves of a restful night with the ever-perplexing questions, "What shall we eat? What shall we drink?"

When these thoughts want to distress us, Jesus bids us remember the promises of God and therefore says: "Neither be ye of doubtful mind." Here we have the cure for worrisome thoughts and misgivings. To put it into a positive statement, Jesus urges us to have faith in God. We should never doubt God and His promises.

Above all we should put our trust in God when Satan tries to frighten us by saying that our sins cannot be forgiven. At such times we should not be of doubtful mind, but cling to the promises which God already made to the people of old: "I have blotted out as a thick cloud thy transgressions and as a cloud thy sins. Return unto Me, for I have redeemed thee," Is. 44, 22.

We have a Father, reconciled through Jesus Christ, who yearns for us and who will ever receive us as we come crying, "Have mercy upon me." None that come to Him will be cast out. Never should we be doubtful about this. In Christ Jesus, God is ever merciful and forgiving and ever ready to help us in all our troubles.

Prayer

We bow our heads to receive Thy benediction, O Lord, in these days of trials and tribulations. We need Thy blessing amid the struggles of our daily life. I need Thee to keep me content and satisfied. I need Thee every hour to resist the sin of doubt and to overcome the vexing worries of the day. Shine Thou into my heart with Thy love and mercy and bless me with Thy forgiveness and peace. Let not the cares of the world burden my heart, but teach me to remember that Thou art opening Thy hand daily and art nigh unto all who call upon Thee.

Bless those who go in and out of this home and fill them with cheerfulness that they may gladly render the service they are called upon to perform. We ask this in the name of Him who has rendered the greatest service to mankind by giving His life to redeem us all, Christ Jesus, our Lord. Amen.

The Anchor That Holds

Which hope we have as an anchor of the soul, both sure and steadfast. — *Heb. 6, 19.*

Every ship has an anchor. The anchors used in the United States Navy often weigh as high as twenty thousand pounds. Before these are fastened to the ship, they are carefully inspected and tested. Men take huge hammers and beat against them. The sailors hoist these anchors to a height of twenty and thirty feet and drop them. Thus they make sure that they are safe.

Every human soul must have an anchor. That anchor is faith. One who has faith stakes his all and all upon some one. When Alexander the Great at one time was sick unto death, he received an unsigned note stating that his physician would offer a new prescription to the king into which the physician had mixed a deadly poison. The letter warned Alexander against taking the medicine. Soon after the king had read the note, the physician entered and announced that he had mixed new herbs, which, he hoped, would cure the king. Alexander took the cup and then handed the note to his physician. While the physician was reading the same, Alexander drank the contents of the cup. By doing this, he wanted to show that he had absolute confidence in his physician. And he did not misplace his confidence. The note was a lie. — That is faith. Such a faith we must have.

This anchor of faith must hold to something. An anchor that is dangling in the water is of no worth. It must be embedded in a rock. The anchor of our soul must be embedded in the Rock of Ages, Jesus Christ, if it is to hold firm and steadfast. If we are anchored to Him, there is nothing in life, in death, or in eternity that can pry us loose. Anchored to Jesus Christ, we are safe amid the storms of life. There are storms within when our conscience accuses us and the finger of guilt says: "Thou art the man," "Thou art the woman." That robs us of sleep. But if we are anchored to Christ, we can find refuge even against our accusing conscience. His blood makes the foulest clean.

Then there are troubles in life. When one evil after the other befalls us like Job, then we are inclined to think that God does not care. But if we hold fast to Jesus Christ, we shall discover that He keeps and preserves us in every sickness and misfortune and at last brings us safely to the haven of eternal life.

What a blessed assurance to know today as we face the critical hour of our life that we can anchor safely in the Rock of Ages and confidently know that this anchor will hold!

Prayer

Merciful God, Thou art with me every hour, even now in this hour of sickness and pain. I ask Thee to abide with me tonight and to relieve me of my suffering and give me a peaceful and restful sleep. Thou hast promised that where two or three are gathered in Thy name and they agree upon one thing to ask of Thee, Thou wilt not turn from them. I ask Thee to be my Keeper, who dost not slumber or sleep. Bless those who watch over me with tender hearts and loving hands and give them and me a faith that will never doubt Thee and Thy promises.

Forgive us where we have sinned against Thee. Glorify Thyself in this hour upon us. Reveal unto us the glory of the cross which tells us of a greater suffering than even ours. May it make us deeply conscious of sin and cause us to hate our iniquities. Hold us close to Thee, so that the Evil Foe may have no power over us. And then may the faith that is within me and the salvation that is mine by grace glorify Thee forever! Through Jesus Christ. Amen.

More Than Conquerors

Who shall separate us from the love of Christ? Shall tribulation, or distress, or persecution, or famine, or nakedness, or peril, or sword? Nay, in all these things we are more than conquerors through Him that loved us. — *Rom. 8, 35. 37.*

God has His heroes as well as the world. But what a different array of names is found in the records of God than in *Who's Who!* In Hebrews eleven the apostle, by divine inspiration, records the names of God's great. It is interesting to study the names of these men. None of them are great in the sight of man. Even Moses and David are not great measured by the standards of the world. Egypt thought Moses a fool, and David is called a leader of a tribal nation. Solomon, whose fame went forth into the world, is not mentioned in Hebrews eleven.

God's heroes fought other battles than those fought with sword and cannon. The woman of Canaan was one of God's great heroines. Jesus says so. "O woman, great is thy faith; be it unto thee even as thou wilt," Matt. 15, 28. But we find no statue reared to her name in Palestine. Yet in God's records her name is one of the foremost. The centurion of Capernaum was one of the great heroes of God. Of him Jesus says: "Verily I say unto you, I have not found so great faith, no, not in Israel," Matt. 8, 10. But no memorial has been reared to this centurion at Capernaum. Paul thought of such when he said: "more than conquerors."

The heroes of God are those who suffer and endure for Christ's sake. The heroes of God are the missionaries who have gone to the ends of the earth, facing danger, enduring hardships, leaving friends and homeland, because of their love for Jesus Christ.

Then there are many unsung heroes in the Christian world of today, who are not enduring persecutions and not facing the sword, but are going through life bearing their trials and burdens and afflictions heroically and uncomplainingly, filled with an unshaken faith in God.

Trouble is common to man. Trouble does not come only to Christians. Trouble also comes to him who has no faith, the atheist, the unbeliever. But when trouble comes to these, they lose hope, they despair, because they have nothing to which they can cling.

But Christian men and women amid their trials and tribulations, amid their afflictions and drawn-out sicknesses, know that they can look hopefully to God with the glorious assurance that the suffering of this world is not worthy to be compared with the glory that awaits them in heaven. They know that no earthly sorrow and trial can separate them from the love of Christ. So they rise above their tribulations and by the grace of God become more than conquerors. They go through life unsung and unpraised, but the Lord knoweth them that are His.

Prayer

Lord, gracious Father, Thou knowest the journey is hard and the trials are great. Yet Thou hast promised Thy continual presence to me and hast assured me through Thy Word sufficient strength for the day. I come to Thee, asking Thee to lift me out of the miry clay of trouble and to set my feet upon a rock, filling me with patience and hope. Let not the trivial irritations of the day rob me of my Christian cheerfulness. Give me grace to remember that my Savior has suffered still greater pain on the cross that He might redeem me for all eternity. Bring to my remembrance His suffering and death and let me find real peace and blessedness in Him.

Be Thou the Keeper of my body and soul every hour of the day and watch over each and every one of us in this home in Thy tender goodness and loving mercy. Keep us all ever faithful to Thy Word. Forgive our sins and remember them no more, but blot them out through the blood of Jesus Christ, our Savior. Amen.

God's Happy People

Happy is that people whose God is the Lord.
Ps. 144, 15.

. The Christian religion is a religion of hope. Therefore it brings joy to the heart. Jesus says: "Rejoice because your names are written in heaven," Luke 10, 20. The angels declared to the shepherds on Bethlehem's plain: "Behold, I bring you good tidings of great joy, which shall be to all people," Luke 2, 10. Therefore the psalmist exclaims: "Happy is that people whose God is the Lord."

However, not all Christians are joyous. Some wear long faces and go through the day with dissatisfied looks. But if Christ has gotten into our heart, we shall rejoice. Paul was able to say: "I have learned in whatsoever state I am therewith to be content," Phil. 4, 11.

You and I ought to be happy Christians because God has assured us that He turns everything to the good of those that love Him. He turns to our good the *dark* things of life. When Joseph was sold into Egypt and there became a slave and then, because he displeased Potiphar's wife, was thrown into the dungeon and there pined away for many years, it did not seem as though God was turning things to his good. Yet all the while God was with Joseph and was planning that he should rise from the dungeon to the throne.

God also turns the *bright* things to the good of those who love Him. Methinks that greater dangers beset us in the days of prosperity and success, comfort and ease, than in the day of adversity. How easily we forget God when all runs well! How indifferent our prayers! How thoughtless our worship! In the good days of life we must know that God is watching over us and is with us to turn everything to our good. Therefore we ought to be happy people of God.

You and I ought to be happy Christians also because God assures us peace of heart and mind through Christ Jesus. We cannot enjoy life if we have no peace of heart. This peace comes to us only through Christ Jesus, who has given His life to reconcile us to the Father. There is no condemnation to those who believe. Their sins are forgiven. They are justified. They are saved. This peace makes us certain that we are heirs of heaven. With Paul we can say that the suffering of this world and the disappointment of this life are not worthy to be compared with the glory that awaits us in eternity. Having this peace fills us with hope.

This peace in our hearts which passes all understanding, and this assurance, that God turns everything to our good, makes us the happy people whose God is the Lord.

Prayer

Gracious Father, I come to Thee because in Thine everlasting arms there is safety. Thou hast assured me Thy continual presence and Thine everlasting peace. Give to me grace to seek refuge with Thee amid the troubles of life and the multitudes of my sins. Forgive me where I have grieved Thee, be it with thought, word, or deed. Fill me with patience every hour of the day and give to me a heart that will be content in whatever state I may be. Let Thy divine presence dwell in the hearts of all who live in this home and keep us all faithful to Thee unto the end. In Jesus' name I ask it. Amen.

"Thy Word"

Thy Word is a lamp unto my feet and a light unto my path.
Ps. 119, 105.

There is only one book in the world that is never off the presses. You know this Book, you have a copy of it in your home, you love it better than any other book — the Bible.

The Bible is the most remarkable Book in the world. You can read and study it for a lifetime, but you cannot outlearn it. It has a message for you, no matter what your temperament and your taste may be, no matter through what trials or sufferings you may pass. To-day you are happy, and you read the 103d Psalm and sing with a greater joy unto the Lord. To-morrow you are troubled and anxious, and you turn to the 14th chapter of St. John's gospel, comforting yourself with these words: "Let not your heart be troubled; ye believe in God, believe also in

Me." The next day your sin comes to your remembrance and wants to drive you to despair. But you turn to the first chapter of Isaiah, where God gives you the blessed assurance: "Come now, let us reason together, saith the Lord. Though your sins be as scarlet, they shall be as white as snow; though they be red like crimson, they shall be as wool."

This wonderful Book is also your unerring guide to heaven. It directs you through life, it helps you to pass through the valley of the shadow of death, and brings you safely to the eternal mansions of the Lord to dwell with Him forever.

The Bible, then, is the guide-book. The psalmist calls this Word a lamp. A lamp is used at night to enable us to read without difficulty. The reading of the Bible gives us a real understanding of life. In the Scriptures are God's revelations, telling us about Himself, about the beginning of all things, and also about the origin of sin and death. Above all the Scriptures make known to us God's wonderful plan of salvation, making us wise through faith in Christ Jesus. The Bible unravels all our twisted ideas and notions and enables us to think straight, to think our thoughts after God.

The psalmist also calls the Bible a light. A light is used to show the way. There is nothing more distressing than losing the trail in the darkness of the night. Spiritually we are blind by nature. We do not know the way to God. The Bible is the light through which the Holy Spirit leads us into the narrow way to life and by which He keeps us on the narrow way in order that we do not get into the mire of sin and into the quicksands of doubt and perish.

A light removes mysteries. In the dark there are often mysterious happenings. Throw on the light, and at once the mysteries disappear. Many things happen in our lives that we cannot explain. We are constantly asking, Why, O Lord? With Gideon we say: "Why, then, is all this befallen us?" But as we turn to the Scriptures, we learn that God turns everything to the good of those that love Him.

This Word never leaves us in the lurch. There is no condition of life, there is no problem so perplexing, but the Scriptures give us some precious assurance, some real help, and some consoling message. This Word never fails us in time of sickness. The Scriptures comfort us in the days when we have lost every human friend. Above all, it is also our stay in the days of prosperity. So the Bible is a sure and certain light, leading us unerringly to eternal life. It tells us that we are sinners, but we can come daily to Christ and be cleansed through His holy, precious blood.

To whom is the Bible a lamp and a light? To all who accept its saving truths. "Whosoever believeth in Him shall not perish," says Christ Jesus.

Search, then, the Scriptures; for God speaks to you through this Book, and in this Word you will find a lamp unto your feet and a light unto your path that leads you to the eternal home in heaven.

Prayer

Lord God, the way that Thou leadest me seems dark. I cannot understand why all this has befallen me. Yet, O Lord, I put my trust in Thee. Though Thou hast sent me into the deep dark valleys of trouble and sorrow and tears, yet I will praise Thee and believe that Thy ways are ways of mercy and of love. Let me not stumble nor fall nor turn from Thee. Strengthen my faith, forgive every sin with which I have offended Thee, and blot it out, and fill me with peace and blessedness of heart and mind.

O Lord, I am in great distress, yet Thou hast promised to be with me even when every other helper fails. Therefore I place myself into Thy hands.

Let Thy Word be precious and dear unto me and to every one in this home. May we by Thy wonderful grace find in it hope, certainty, and salvation. These our petitions we bring to Thee in the name of Thy Son Jesus Christ, our Lord. Amen.

He Leads Me with a Shepherd's Care

He shall feed His flock like a shepherd; He shall gather the lambs with His arm and carry them in His bosom and shall gently lead those that are with young. — *Is. 40, 11.*

We all need shepherding. Sheep, of all creatures, are the most helpless and defenseless. They easily wander away from the flock and are beset on all sides by dangers, especially in the open stretches, on the mountainsides, and in the deep ravines. Therefore they need shepherding. We Christians are like sheep. We cannot by our own power and strength remain with the Good Shepherd. We have three master enemies, the devil, the world, and our flesh, who are ever seeking to destroy our souls. Therefore we need shepherding.

God gives us the heartening assurance in His Word that our Good Shepherd "shall lead His flock like a shepherd." Because you and I are often discouraged as we go through life, we need this reassuring promise, that the Good Shepherd watches over us with His tenderest care.

As first promise He gives us the assurance that He shall feed His flock. He leads us into the green pastures of His Word, where the soul is nourished. He leads His flock to the still waters and refreshes our drooping souls and revives them. The Gospel soothes, comforts, quiets, and calms. Sin is forgiven. Strength is promised. Every need of the soul is satisfied through this Word.

The second promise which emerges from the text gives

us the assurance that "He shall gather the lambs with His arm and carry them in His bosom." The lambs are the weak, those who have little strength; the inexperienced, who know not what to do; the stupid, who often blunder; the frisky, who do foolish things. Such weak, inexperienced, stupid, and light-hearted men and women are always getting into tight places and endangering their souls. They therefore need the Good Shepherd to protect and defend them.

The third promise that comes forth from the text tells us that "He shall gently lead those that are with young." Here the Lord is thinking of the bruised. They have lost the battle, and they know it. They have fought and have been defeated. Their souls are bruised and blackened because they have been conquered by sin. Their conscience hurts. The sting of guilt is upon them. Life seems hard and bitter to them.

Then there are Christians who are troubled. Into their lives have come misfortunes. They have one spell of sickness after another. They are often unable to work and therefore are in want.

Then there are those who are perplexed. They cannot understand God's ways. Why should so many wrongs go unpunished? Why should the Christian suffer while the ungodly seem to go scot-free? Why should youth die and the aged and the helpless live?

To these bruised, troubled, and perplexed the Good Shepherd says that He shall gently lead them. The bruised He heals. He will make them whole. He restoreth their souls. The troubled He quiets. He invites them to come unto Him and find rest. The perplexed He shows the way. "Thomas, come hither," said Jesus to the disciple whose mind was in a whirl. Thomas places the finger into His hand and then touches the open side, and lo! he no longer is faithless, but believing.

Truly, the Shepherd cares. This means much to you and to me. Every fear is removed from the heart. Every doubt is taken away. I know that there is a Rock that is higher than I, a Haven to which I can safely sail, a Refuge to which I can go for shelter. This blessed assurance makes me hopeful in the day of sickness and in the day of trouble. I have a Shepherd who leads me daily and all the way.

Prayer

Thou art my Shepherd, O Lord, and therefore I shall not want as long as I abide in the green pastures of Thy Word. Keep me faithful. Refresh me today and feed me that my soul may wax fat upon Thy promises. Thou knowest, O Lord, that often I am discouraged and disheartened. Thou knowest how vexing are my problems and how trying my sufferings. But I put my trust in Thee. I know that Thou art with me to redeem my life from destruction. Let it please Thee, O Lord, to give me the desires of my heart. Therefore I place myself and all those who dwell with me in this home into Thy loving hands, trusting that Thy mercy and goodness shall see us safely through the day. Strengthen Thou my faith through the Lord Jesus Christ. Amen.

God Supplies Every Need

My God shall supply all your need according to His riches in glory by Christ Jesus. — *Phil. 4, 19.*

We do not know what the future holds in store for us, whether joy or sorrow, health or sickness, life or death. Not two of us will have just the same experience, for not two of us are alike. Every one differs from every other person in the world. They tell us that not even one leaf is like the other on a single tree.

Some things we hold in common: sorrow and tears, joy and love, worries and cares, and death. But many of the things that we are wont to worry about never come to pass. They rise like ghosts in the night to frighten us. Many of our worries are like scarecrows which we find in the garden, looking dangerous and yet being harmless.

We Christians can look forward confidently because Paul assures us: "My God shall supply all your need." Over against every gloomy outlook of life Paul gives us here the secret of overcoming and enjoying a care-free life. Paul reached into his pockets, and he found them empty. Yet he is confident that he will never want. He does not know where his bread is coming from tomorrow, but he does know that God has promised him food, clothing, and shelter. This same confidence you and I should have.

"My God shall supply all your need," our physical need. He gives us all that we need for the support and want of our body. He defends us against all danger. He guards and protects us daily. He watches over us in the day of sickness. He gently leads us who are in trouble.

"My God shall supply all your need," our spiritual need. He will abundantly pardon. He forgives the iniquity of our sin. He creates in us a clean heart and renews a right spirit within us. He restores unto us the joy of salvation. He also promises to answer our prayer. He gives us everlasting life.

All this He gives us "according to His riches in glory by Jesus Christ." We have not deserved it. We are unworthy of His help. We are undeserving of His forgiveness. But His love in Christ Jesus is so great, so wide, so all-embracing, that it reaches down to you and me and supplies all our needs.

Truly, we can be glad in the Lord and shout for joy. We can praise Him, for He is our Refuge and Strength, a very present Help in trouble. Trusting in His promises, we should believe that He will gloriously supply all our needs.

Prayer

Heavenly Father, I approach Thy throne through Jesus Christ, my Savior, asking Thee to guide me with Thine eye and to abide with me every hour of the day. I need Thee, for without Thee I fail and perish. Be Thou my Strength in the hour of weakness, my Light in the moment of darkness, my Shepherd in the day of trouble, my Comforter in my sorrows and tears, my divine Healer of all my sin.

Give me grace to be faithful to Thee, courage to confess Thee, and strength to hold fast to Thy promises. Fill my heart with the joy of forgiveness. Teach me to be content and patient in my afflictions.

Let our home be Thy temple, and dwell Thou in our midst. O Thou eternal Caretaker, who hast never forsaken me in the day of trouble, uphold me with Thy everlasting arms and keep me and all that are mine faithful to Jesus Christ, our Lord, unto death. Amen.

Staggering Promises

He staggered not at the promise of God through unbelief, but was strong in faith, giving glory to God and being fully persuaded that what He had promised He was able also to perform. And therefore it was imputed to him for righteousness.
Rom. 4, 20—22.

The Bible is God's Book, open for all men. Every one who will may read it. In this Book of books God makes promises that stagger the imagination. These promises are of a twofold nature, such as pertain to our physical well-being and those pertaining to our soul's salvation.

God made some staggering promises to His people of old. He told Abraham to go out into the night and gaze at the stars of heaven to count them. Abraham could not number the lights of heaven. God said to him: "So shall thy seed be." A lonely man and wife come to Palestine and are promised to have millions and millions of descendants. Abraham staggered not, but believed.

To you and to me God has given promises equally

great. He says: "I will never leave thee nor forsake thee."
Again: "Commit thy way unto the Lord, trust also in Him,
and He shall bring it to pass." Again: "And it shall come
to pass that, before they call, I will answer, and while they
are yet speaking, I will hear." Once more: "To him that
worketh not, but believeth on Him that justifieth the ungodly, his faith is counted for righteousness." Joshua
therefore at the close of his life declares that not one of
the promises of God had failed him. That holds true
to this day.

When Abraham heard the promise of God, he staggered not. His faith was not handicapped by unbelief and
doubt. No matter what man said and how man argued,
Abraham believed God. Such a faith laughs at mountains,
overcomes difficulties, and believes that God can do what
He has promised. Such a faith remains unshaken in the
day of trouble and cannot be overthrown by the ever-
changing problems of life.

Such a faith, which believes the promises of God under
all conditions, shall not go without reward. To Abraham
this faith was imputed for righteousness. This faith was
counted and credited to Abraham in lieu of perfection and
sinlessness. This faith gave Abraham the assurance of
heaven. Let us, then, ask God to give us a faith that will
never stagger at His promises, but, believing His Word,
cling to them even though everything seems contrary.

Prayer

Lord, Thy promises are new to me every morning. Wherever I turn in Thy Word, Thou art promising to me some blessing and some gift by Thy wonderful graces. Bless me with
a childlike faith, so that I will accept these promises even though
I cannot understand and know how Thou wilt fulfil them to me.
I am undeserving of these blessings because so often I have
sinned against Thee and ignored Thee in the days when Thou
didst bless me. Lord, I am ashamed of myself; but hide not

Thy face from me. Blot out again all my sins and receive me
into Thy grace and into Thy love. Give me the strength to love
Thee with a deeper love, to follow Thee with a fuller devotion,
and to serve Thee with a greater faithfulness. Help me to overcome every doubt and believe Thy promises. Be Thou my Stay
in the hour of trial and in the moments of temptation. Help me
to overcome my unbelief and keep me steadfast and faithful to
my Lord Jesus Christ. Amen.

The Upward Look

But the God of all grace, who hath called us unto His eternal
glory, . . . strengthen you. — *1 Pet. 5, 10.*

We Christians are traveling toward the eternal glory
of heaven. Eternity is a momentous word. We cannot
grasp the full meaning of it. Our mind staggers when we
begin to reckon with eternity. Never ending; think what
it means — never ending! When a million years are over,
eternity has only begun. That makes many fear death, for
they do not know what awaits them in eternity.

The Christian is not afraid. He knows what eternity
holds for him. The God of all grace has called him to his
eternal glory through the redemption of Jesus Christ. Since
we do not know, however, when we are going home to this
glory, we should always keep ourselves in readiness.

We are always to have our house set in order. We are
to have the affairs of our life arranged in such a fashion
that we can depart at a moment's notice.

Setting our house in order, we will ever seek to live at
peace with all mankind. Being at peace with God, we
shall want to be at peace also with man. If, therefore, we
remember that some one has aught against us, we will at
once endeavor to be reconciled.

Setting our house in order means that we will make
certain of our soul's salvation. We will give first thought
to spiritual things. We will assure ourselves of God's

peace and forgiveness through the Word and the Sacrament. Through these we shall be strengthened and kept unto the day of our Lord and Savior Jesus Christ.

Every Christian should live each day as though it were his last day on earth. We have here no abiding city. We live in the world, but are not of the world. We live to the glory of God. Living such consecrated lives will draw others unto Christ and keep us prepared and waiting for the eternal glory that is to come.

Prayer

Our times are in Thy hand, O Lord Jesus; therefore I fear no evil. Thou hast redeemed my soul from destruction. Surely Thou wouldst not forsake me in the day of sickness. I come to Thee because Thou art my Help and my Strength and my sure Defense. Bless the physician that waits upon me and give him wisdom and understanding. Bless the medicine that he prescribes. Above all heal Thou my soul from sin and give me the blessed assurance through Thy Word and Sacrament that all is well for time and eternity as long as Thou dost watch over me. Into Thy hands I place myself and all that are mine. Thou hast redeemed us, Lord Jesus. Amen.

"Hold Fast!"

Hold that fast which thou hast that no man take thy crown.
Rev. 3, 11.

Hold fast to Jesus Christ. He is the only Savior who really saves. Others may promise to help you out of your sin, but there is none other that can pay the price which redeems souls but Jesus, God's Son become flesh. Without Him we cannot obtain the crown of life, for He has purchased salvation with His blood. Satan ever and again holds out to us wonderful inducements. He is willing to promise us anything. But the end is always death. Now, we cannot hold fast to the Lord Jesus Christ and to the devil. We either serve the one, or we serve the other. But if we want the crown of life, we must hold fast to Jesus Christ.

Hold fast to the promises of Jesus. Jesus promises forgiveness. He will wash away all your sins. With our sins blotted out, we can stand in the judgment of God unafraid, for we are clothed in the righteousness of our Savior. This fills us with peace and contentment in this world; for, believing the promises of our Lord, we need not fear the future, as heaven is our home. Therefore we want to hold fast to the promises of Jesus.

Hold fast to the Word of Jesus. The Bible is that Word. This Word instructs us on all questions of life and eternity. This Word serves as a compass and therefore keeps the ship of life on the right path as we travel the trackless ocean of this world. Our ship of life will strike rocks and shoals and sand-banks unless this Word directs us. The Bible is our spiritual compass. As long as we follow the instructions of this Book of books, we are safe. Therefore we want to hold fast to this Word of Jesus.

To those who hold fast Jesus promises the crown of everlasting life.

Prayer

Thou, most merciful God, hast made us kings and princes of Thy glorious kingdom through Jesus Christ. Thou hast given me a name more glorious than any name in the world. Thou hast called me to be a Christian. Grant that I may always be worthy of this exalted name and at last by Thy wonderful grace receive the crown of everlasting life.

Grant that I may at no time dishonor this name, which is mine by grace, by ungodly conversation, by unbelief and doubt, by anxious cares and useless fretting. Wherever I have sinned, blot out these sins and create through Thy Holy Spirit faith in Thy Word, so that I shall never doubt Thy promises. Make me a better Christian day by day. Keep before my eyes the Lord Jesus, who has died for me, and let His undying love incite me to greater love for Him who has loved me first. Grant this of Thy mercy and love for Jesus' sake. Amen.

Refined in the Furnace

Behold, I have refined thee, but not with silver; I have chosen thee in the furnace of affliction. — *Is. 48, 10.*

Trouble touches every human life. Physically, trouble touches us through sickness, pain, and affliction. Mentally, trouble comes through worry and heartaches. Spiritually, trouble comes through a guilty conscience, doubt, and distrust.

We see trouble on all sides — in the hospitals, in the homes, in the jails, and in reform schools.

Trouble only comes to us because of the sinfulness of the human race. There are natural and moral consequences of sinning. The natural consequences are pain, aches, suffering, and death. The spiritual consequences of sin are the sense of guilt, the spiritual death of the soul, and eternal death.

The guilt and blame of sin is removed for the Christian through forgiveness. The message of the Cross tells us that Christ gave His life in exchange for ours. He became our Substitute. So we can escape completely the eternal death; for Christ has made full satisfaction for our sins with His blood, and so we are at peace with our God.

Trouble comes into the lives of Christians and often is a blessing is disguise. Trouble is painful and grievous, but by it and through it the soul is saved. Therefore our text tells us that God chooses to send us into the furnace of affliction to refine and to cleanse our soul.

This refining of the soul brings out our real worth. It reveals to us what we are by the grace of God and develops in us Christian virtues, such as patience, cheerfulness, hope, and trust.

This refining of our soul also makes us weary of this world. We are ready to depart and to be with Christ.

This is not the case when all goes well. Then we are more likely to cling to this world and to love its pleasures. When God wanted to take Israel out of Egypt, He had the Egyptians oppress them. They then sighed for deliverance and were eager to get out of the land. Pain makes us cry out for deliverance in our distress. In the day of adversity we pray, Lord, take us home!

In the furnace of affliction we are led to seek refuge, strength, and comfort in the right place; we will go to God in prayer; we will study the Scriptures that its wonderful promises may encourage us.

So the Christian goes into the furnace of affliction by the will of God. "I have chosen thee in the furnace of affliction." But when God chooses to refine us, He is with us and is for us. Therefore He turns everything to the good of those that love Him. Such promises make us hopeful, cheerful, and courageous.

What do troubles mean to you? They may be stumbling-blocks, and then they lead you into despair. However, your troubles should be stepping-stones that lead you to heaven.

Prayer

Jesus, Lover of my soul,
    Let me to Thy bosom fly
While the waters nearer roll,
    While the tempest still is high!
Hide me, O my Savior, hide,
    Till the storm of life is past;
Safe into the haven guide;
    O receive my soul at last! Amen.

Praying for Wings

Oh, that I had wings like a dove! For then would I fly away
and be at rest. — *Ps. 55, 6.*

We are living in a very restless age. We rush from one
thing to another. We hasten through the day, hardly taking time to eat and snatching only a few moments of sleep
in the wee hours of the night. We are always on the go
and are unhappy if we cannot run from one place to
another.

What makes this age so restless? Certainly not the
creation of God. The sun does not travel any faster today
than it did two thousand years ago. The year is just as
long in the twentieth century as it was in the eighteenth.
It takes an elm just as long to grow today as in the days
of Washington. The child does not grow into maturity
any sooner than it did in the days of Lincoln.

Man makes this age restless. Man always has been
restless. There is in the heart of man a desire to get away.
The migration of nations, the clearing of the jungles, the
explorations of the pioneers, the slow journeys of the
covered wagons in our country, all tell the story of man's
restlessness. We want to get away from our present sur-
roundings.

Some want wings of a dove because they are tired of
their tasks. Others want wings of a dove because they are
weary of the daily routine. Others want wings of a dove
because they want to get away from under the burdens of
the day and the troubles of the hour.

David believed, for a time at least, that he could find
rest if he could get away from his neighbors, from his sur-
roundings, from slandering tongues, from the burden of
his office, from the problems of his home, and above all
from his sins and transgressions. Men and women think
that they can run away from their responsibilities. No
one, however, has found rest this way.

David learned the lesson. He discovered that he could
not find rest by running from place to place. Only at one
place could he find real contentment, and therefore he said
at the close of this psalm: "Cast thy burden upon the
Lord, and He shall sustain thee." Only in Christ and
through Christ can we find rest and peace. That is why
Jesus says: "Come unto Me, all ye that labor and are
heavy laden, and I will give you rest," Matt. 11, 28.

Prayer

Wonderful Savior, whither can I go but to Thee to find rest
for my soul? Going hither and thither, seeking peace, I find
none. Therefore I come to Thee because Thou dost ask the
weary and the heavy laden to come. I am weary. The trials of
life oppress me. I am discouraged and disheartened.

I am heavy laden with sin, with failings, with shortcomings.
I have not always loved Thee, I have not always sought strength
in Thee. Here I am. Take me, with all my burdens of body and
soul, into Thy bosom and comfort me, strengthen me, forgive me,
and heal me. Amen.

"Comfort Ye My People!"

Now, our Lord Jesus Christ Himself and God, even our Father,
which hath loved us and hath given us everlasting consolation and
good hope through grace, comfort your hearts.
2 Thess. 2, 16. 17.

God always speaks hopefully to the Christians. He
always has a message of cheer for those who are in trouble.
From cover to cover the Bible speaks encouragingly to
God's children. Because the Scriptures offer hope to all in
Christ, that is why the Christian religion is so comforting.
God is a God of comfort. Whatever may be the situation
in life, God always has a message that lifts man out of
despair.

The Christian religion comforts because it gives peace
against sin. Sin is universal, and so is conscience. For some

sins, restitution can be made, in a measure, with men. Some
sins, however, can never be undone. In the sight of God,
however, no sin can be atoned for by man. How, then,
can man find peace? The Word answers: God removes
sin through Christ. Jesus took upon Himself the load of
sin and paid the price. Thus our Christian faith comforts us. "Be of good cheer; thy sin is forgiven thee."

Our Christian religion comforts because it offers a
refuge to us in the day of trouble. Christian faith does not
exempt us from trouble. These troubles are trying. Ever
and again the voice of Satan is heard within, whispering to
us doubts about the goodness and the justice of God. Our
Christian faith offers us refuge in trouble. The Bible assures us that we have a personal God, who neither slumbers
nor sleeps. Our Christian faith gives us something to lean
upon: Believe on Jesus. Thus we are comforted, as the
Lord Jesus says: "Let not your heart be troubled, neither
let it be afraid."

Our Christian religion comforts because it fills us with
hope in the hour of death. Death is universal. Death is
the penalty for sin. By nature all dread the thought of
death. The Christian, however, has no fear because for
him death is the gateway to heaven. Jesus says to us Christians: "Because I live, ye shall live also."

This glorious hope, which comforts our heart, is ours
through grace. God has loved us and therefore has given
us this consolation, which never fails. Therefore we need
not be afraid to face the day and the troubles of the day.

Prayer

Lord God, Keeper of my body and Keeper of my soul, I fly
to Thee for refuge. Satan sorely besets me with doubt and with
fear. Let him not have power over my thoughts. Drive him out
of my heart and give me grace to cling to Thy promise. Lord,
Thou knowest how discouraged I often become. I sink, I faint,

I fall. Stretch forth Thy helping hand. Let me nestle safely in the sunshine of Thy love. Above all make me content and satisfied. Grant that those who wait upon me will cheerfully render the service which is required. Forgive my sins and remember them no more. I ask all this because of Him who has given His life to save me, Christ Jesus, my Lord. Amen.

Whom Does Jesus Help?

They that be whole need not a physician, but they that are sick. — *Matt. 9, 12.*

Jesus came into the world to save the human race from its sin-sickness. However, many cannot be helped by Jesus because they will not admit that they are sick at heart. Therefore they spurn the kindly hand of Jesus, the Great Physician, who wants to heal their souls. The Pharisees of Jesus' day were such as believed that all was well with them, that they had never done any wrong, and that their souls were not bespotted with sin. Such Jesus cannot help.

What kind of people does Jesus heal? "They that are sick." Some of these are altogether broken in spirit, others are bruised, still others are bent. To these Jesus comes with the healing power of the Gospel and binds up their broken hearts and lifts them out of their sinfulness. He eases their hearts and minds by cleansing them from sin and filling them with peace from on high.

Jesus will help also those who are downcast, depressed, and discouraged. He shows them that they are pilgrims and strangers in this world who are journeying to heaven, where sorrows and tears and heartache find no place, but the fulness of joy in God abideth forever.

Jesus helps those who are troubled in conscience and therefore can find no rest day or night. There is no herb that can heal its sting. All Neptune's water cannot wash away the guilt. But Jesus does cleanse the conscience and makes possible our acquittal at the judgment-throne of God. Thus He heals those who are sick at heart because of their many sins and transgressions.

Today Jesus is still the Great Physician of the world. He stands in the midst of mankind as the sinners' only hope. If Jesus is not your Savior, then you have no Savior. And the glory of it all is this, that none who come to Him are sent away uncured. He helps every one who comes to Him in his troubles of body or soul or mind. Whether you are like the bruised reed or the smoking flax, Jesus can help you, Jesus can heal you, and Jesus can save you.

Prayer

Merciful Savior, look down upon me and behold my pain and help me in my distress. Thou art full of mercy and tender compassion and art acquainted with all my needs. Without Thee, O Lord, I perish.

My times are in Thy hand, and therefore I fear no evil; for Thou art able to preserve and keep those who put their trust in Thee. Thou hast redeemed me from all sins and hast rescued me from the destruction of eternal death. Therefore I put myself into Thy hands and as a child trust in Thy mercy, knowing that Thy love for me is greater than that of a mother.

Let me not doubt Thy promises nor question Thy power to help. Fill me with patience to wait for Thy appointed time. As the Great Physician of my soul cleanse me from every sin and blot out every transgression. Give me strength to believe day after day, so that I may rise above every discouragement that wants to distress my soul.

Be Thou very near to every one who dwells in this home and bless Thy Church and the preaching of Thy Gospel everywhere. Amen.

"Jesus, Savior, Pilot Me"

But the ship was now in the midst of the sea, tossed with waves; for the wind was contrary. And in the fourth watch of the night Jesus went unto them, walking on the sea.
Matt. 14, 24. 25.

Life is an adventure and has often been compared to the going out upon the unknown sea. The trackless waters, the hidden shoals, the sudden storms, are pictures of the trials, tribulations, and hardships which we meet on life's voyage. Today all is calm, and tomorrow it seems as though we should perish. Often we start out with an ideal day, and before we come to the sunset hour, we are facing contrary winds and find the day full of trouble and full of anguish.

So we begin to pray. Blessed is the man and blessed the woman who, traveling over life's tempestuous sea, have learned to pray: "Jesus, Savior, pilot me."

If we were compelled to face these big winds alone, we should be at our wit's end; for sin comes to our remembrance, and we have no excuse to give. We must admit our guilt. In those hours doubt likewise assails the heart. We wonder whether God really loves us and cares.

But we are only at our wit's end as we face the contrary winds until Jesus comes into our lives. As sin accuses us, Jesus shows us His pierced hands and open side. These tell us that He was wounded for our transgressions. He brings into our hearts perfect peace by washing away all our sins.

When trouble wants to crush us, Jesus comes into our life as our Strength and Power. In spite of every contrary wind He guides us. There is no night so dark into which Jesus does not come to drive away despair and hopelessness.

The Christian therefore is not at his wit's end when he faces the big winds of trouble of body and soul. He knows that his Lord Jesus Christ is at the helm of his life's ship, guiding and directing him and bringing him safely to the haven of eternity.

Thus we must learn to trust, not in ourselves, but in the Lord Jesus. But if we trust in Him, we shall also pray. In the hour of trial we shall seek the Lord. We shall go into His Word and learn of His promises.

When we are facing the big winds of life, let us go to Christ Jesus, our Savior and Friend, trusting in His mercy and believing His promises.

Prayer

Lord Jesus, Captain of my soul, guide and lead me safely through the day. Thou knowest the troubles that are heaped upon me; Thou art acquainted with my suffering and pain. Lord, I have no strength. Therefore I come to Thee. Protect me today against sin and doubt. Preserve my life in this hour of sickness. Let me know that Thou art with me in the daytime and dost tenderly watch over me throughout the night. Wash me thoroughly from all my sins. Therefore I place myself into Thy loving care throughout the day and throughout the night.

> Jesus, Savior, pilot me
>   Over life's tempestuous sea;
> Unknown waves before me roll,
>   Hiding rock and treacherous shoal;
> Chart and compass came from Thee:
> Jesus, Savior, pilot me.

Better than a Sheep

And He said unto them, What man shall there be among you that shall have one sheep and, if it fall into a pit on the Sabbath, will not lay hold on it and lift it out? How much, then, is a man better than a sheep! — *Matt. 12, 11. 12.*

How much are you worth? Life at times has been dirt-cheap. When the proud kings of Egypt sought to make themselves a name never to be forgotten, they compelled more than a hundred thousand men to build the pyramids.

Men were harnessed to their task and driven like cattle under the whip of the taskmaster, and they died like flies. Thank God we have a higher estimate of life and place a higher value upon a human soul today.

Jesus always valued man highly. He tells us that a child is priceless when He declares: "Whoso shall offend one of these little ones which believe in Me, it were better for him that a millstone were hanged about his neck, and that he were drowned in the depth of the sea," Matt. 18, 6. In our text, Jesus tells us that a man is better than a sheep.

But why is man better than a sheep in the sight of God? The creation of man gives the answer. The Sacred Record says: "And the Lord God formed man of the dust of the ground and breathed into his nostrils the breath of life, and man became a living soul," Gen. 2, 7. This soul lifts man above the sheep. Man is not merely created for this life, but for life eternal.

Man is better than the sheep not merely because God, by creating him as He did, placed him above the sheep, but because, after man had sinned, God redeemed him through His Son Jesus Christ, who went to the cross and with His holy, precious blood purchased us from sin, from death, and from the power of the devil. That God sent His only-begotten Son to redeem us with His blood shows that man is indeed better than a sheep.

To us this brings untold comfort. God is good to the sheep. He provides grass and pasturage for the sheep and clothes it in woolen fleece to keep it warm against the wind and the snow. If God is good to the sheep, then He certainly will take care of you and of me. He will give us all that we need to preserve this body and life.

God will take care of us spiritually. The very fact that the Gospel is preached to us shows that God loves us. He feeds us with this manna from heaven day after day. This nourishes our soul. Doubt and fear cannot take hold of us. By His grace we have the strength to overcome every enemy of our soul. Truly, we want to thank God that we are better than a sheep in His sight, children, once lost, but now redeemed and saved by God's wonderful grace through the blood of Jesus Christ.

Prayer

Lord, heavenly Father, I approach Thy throne of mercy through Jesus Christ, my Lord, who has atoned for the sins of the world with His precious blood, and plead with Thee to give me strength for the day and preserve me from every harm and danger. Thou hast made me Thine own and promised Thy divine presence in the day of trouble. Lord, I need Thee. Forgive me wherever I have sinned against Thee and graciously protect me from doubt and unbelief, worry and care. Bless the physician that is waiting upon me and those who tenderly take care of me in this home. Fill us with cheerfulness and give us courage to carry on. I ask this in Jesus' name. Amen.

Past Finding Out

There be three things which are too wonderful for me.
Prov. 30, 18.

Solomon tells us of three things that are so wonderful to him that he has never ceased to marvel: the way of an eagle in the air; the way of a serpent upon a rock; the way of a ship in the midst of the sea.

What would Solomon say if he were to return to this world and behold the wonderful things that you and I are privileged to see: the X-ray, the radio, and the airship?

But there are things even far more wonderful than these. They are found in the spiritual realm. But many, having eyes, do not observe them.

We marvel at God's wonderful dealings with man. This is far more wonderful than the way of the eagle in the air or the way of a ship in the midst of the sea. With a firm hand He leads the nations, as we may readily observe when we read the history of Israel. Gently He leads the individual, as we learn when we study the life of Abraham and read the Book of Esther. God guides also you and me. He promises: "I will guide thee with Mine eye."

We marvel likewise at God's unsearchable judgments. Saul is chosen as king of Israel, but, disobedient to God, goes down into despair and death. David, falling into scarlet sins, is lifted out of his transgression and saved. Again, the old live, and the young die, the wicked prosper for a time, and the Christians suffer. Why is all this? We look through a glass, darkly. It is all mystery. But there is no darkness around the throne of God. Though the ways of God are not our ways and His judgments are past finding out, nevertheless God has a reason for His every act and a plan for every life.

We also marvel when we behold God's method of saving souls. Man's means of conquest are sword, battleship, army, airship. Man's methods are propaganda, shouting, cults, heresy. God's method is the foolishness of preaching, as Scripture itself declares. God saves man by grace and not by works. This is too wonderful for us, nevertheless gloriously true.

But above all we marvel at the atonement, that God sends His Son into the world, who by the shedding of His blood pays the ransom-price. Christ died for us while we were yet sinners. This seems too wonderful when we think of the dying thief, of the woman who was a sinner, and many others. But the blood of Jesus Christ can make the foulest clean. The blood of Jesus Christ must cleanse also you and me if we are to have peace and to be filled with hope. Daily God offers to cleanse us through His Gospel.

These are the most wonderful things in the world, and we want to thank God that He has brought us to the knowledge of these things, which comfort and save you and me.

Prayer

I thank Thee, most gracious Lord, that Thou hast called me out of darkness into the glorious light of the Gospel of Jesus Christ. Bless me with a love that will never wane. Strengthen my faith and confirm my resolutions to be more faithful. Show me Thy ways and let me learn that they are good and gracious, merciful and gentle. Remember not the sins of my youth nor my many transgressions. Turn not from me in the days of trouble, but bring me out of my distresses. Look upon my affliction and forgive all my sins.

Let not the deceiving cults of today confuse my mind and rob me of the Lord Jesus Christ as my Savior.

Into Thy tender care I place myself and all those who are in this home. Teach us ever to remember Thy goodness of old and Thy tender mercies. Preserve Thine altar in our home and bless us in body and soul and for time and eternity, for Jesus' sake. Amen.

The Eternal Caretaker

Casting all your care upon Him, for He careth for you.
1 Pet. 5, 7.

God is our eternal Caretaker. He has the affairs of the world in His hands and sets the boundaries for the nations. Sometimes it seems as though everything were turned topsy-turvy in this world, as though there were no guiding hand to direct the lives of men. Nevertheless God guides the affairs of the world, of the nations, and of the Church. Nothing happens without His will nor without His permission.

God is your eternal Caretaker. He gives you all that you need to support your body and life. As His child you enjoy His loving guidance. As you look back upon the history of your life, you cannot fail to note that God has walked with you all the way. Not even a sparrow falls to the ground without His permission. How much less shall anything befall you against the will of your heavenly Father?

God is the eternal Caretaker of your soul. He has saved you. Christ came into the world for this purpose, that He might redeem you from the bondage of Satan and free you from the curse of sin and make you heir of His eternal kingdom. Daily God puts a hedge about you, protecting you from temptations, false prophets, and doubt.

God is the Caretaker of us all, the greatest as well as the smallest, the mighty as well as the weak. He does not only take care of a Moses in the bulrushes, of a Paul in the Philippi prison, of an Elijah at the brook. There is no child of God living over whom our heavenly Father does not watch with His tenderest care and undying love.

If God is the eternal Caretaker of His people, then you should cast all your cares and worries upon Him. Be anxious about nothing. Not only the big things that want to worry you, but also the trifling, little, insignificant vexations of the day you should bring to Him in prayer.

If you cast all your care upon the eternal Caretaker, then you can look into the future fearlessly and hopefully.

Prayer

I thank Thee, heavenly Father, through Jesus Christ, for Thy wonderful protection given me day after day. Thy mercies have been new each day. I ask Thee to be with me today, protecting me from all dangers and guarding me from the snares of Satan and the world. Lead me into ways that are acceptable to Thee.

I come to Thee, heavenly Father, placing myself and all who are in this home into Thy divine hands as the eternal Caretaker of our bodies and of our souls. Strengthen us for the tasks of the day and guide us with Thine eye. Let Thy holy angels surround us that Satan and sin may have no power over us. We ask this because of Him who has gone to the cross to redeem us — Jesus, our Savior. Amen.

No Need of Worrying

It is vain for you to rise up early, to sit up late, to eat the bread of sorrows; for so He giveth His beloved sleep. — *Ps. 127, 2.*

Worry is one of the world's greatest trouble-makers. Worry robs us of sleep and takes from us our appetite, so that we eat our bread in sorrow. Worry makes us ask day after day: What shall we eat? Wherewith shall we be clothed? Who will take care of me in old age? These thoughts come to us especially in the days of sickness. These thoughts molest the shut-ins and the invalids. Worry causes us to toss about restlessly at night and vexes our soul and body.

As Christians we have no right to worry, for we have a heavenly Father whose loving-kindness and tender mercies embrace us every day. Out of the fulness of our hearts we should rather pray: "Thy will be done; give us this day our daily bread," and then confidently believe that God will provide for our every need.

God can take care of us in an unusual way. He can provide for us by miracle. Elijah was fed by the ravens. Israel was given manna in the wilderness. The five thousand had enough and to spare on five barley-loaves. As a rule, God uses the natural means to provide bread. He gives rain and sunshine in due season and commands us to gather the grain in the sweat of our brow. God has decreed that through work our daily bread should come to us. Therefore the apostle says to the Thessalonian Christians: "If any would not work, neither should he eat; for we hear that there are some which walk among you disorderly, working not at all, but are busybodies. Now, them that are such we command and exhort by our Lord Jesus Christ that with quietness they work and eat their own bread," 2 Thess. 3, 10—12.

Since God takes care of us day after day, therefore

the psalmist declares by inspiration: "It is vain," that is, foolish, "to rise up early, to sit up late, to eat the bread of sorrows." All the worrying that you do will not make things better. Through your worrying you tell God that you do not trust Him. You are not casting all your care upon Him, but are trying to carry the burden alone. That is foolish and gets us nowhere.

True, it is not easy to set aside our worries. No physician, no herb, no science, can cure you of worry. The only remedy is faith in God. The Lord has adopted you into His family at your baptism and at that time made a covenant with you to be a Father unto you. Therewith He assured you that He would take care of you for time and for eternity. "Fear thou not, for I am with thee; be not dismayed, for I am thy God. I will strengthen thee; yea, I will help thee; yea, I will uphold thee with the right hand of My righteousness," Is. 41, 10.

As worrisome thoughts try to vex you, go to your God in prayer and confidently tell Him of all your needs and wants. Then leave the rest to Him and sleep the peaceful sleep of His beloved.

Prayer

To Thy throne of grace I come in my distress, O Lord, because of Jesus Christ, my Savior, and plead with Thee that Thou wouldst fill my heart with that peace which passeth all understanding. O Lord, I am greatly distressed. The cares of life weigh heavily upon me. My sins are also ever before me. With all my vexing burdens I come to Thee and place them at Thy feet, O Lord, and ask Thee that Thou wouldst give me the grace to leave Thy throne-room with the song of joy upon my lips. Give to me days of peace and nights of rest. Blot out all my sins and remember them no more.

Let not the cares of the world and the anxieties for the morrow find room in our home. As we rise in the early morning, prepare our hearts to be temples of Thine wherein Thou mayest dwell.

Bring each one of the loved ones day after day into the safety

of this home to gather at the family altar for prayer and praise
made unto Thee. Let Thy Word dwell in us richly and teach
us in all Thy wisdom from on high that with psalms and hymns
and spiritual songs we may sing Thy praises now and forever. In
Jesus' name we ask it. Amen.

God's Guiding Eye

I will instruct thee and teach thee in the way which thou shalt
go; I will guide thee with Mine eye. — *Ps. 32, 8.*

There is much uncertainty in this world. We Christians, however, are certain of one thing, the guidance of
God. God does not fail to be with us and to lead us into
the ways that we should go. This He does through His
Word, which is unerring and sure. If, then, we are to be
certain that we are on the right road, we want to follow
daily the instructions given in the Scriptures. This Word
never fails us.

We are not dependent upon superstitious omens, nor
are we to trust in dreams or hope for special visions. God
has given us His Word, and this Word shall stand forever
and ever. Even heaven and earth shall pass away, but
"My words," says Jesus, "shall not pass away."

Through this Word He leads us into the paths of
righteousness. Daily we are face to face with temptations
and sin. The devil is ever eager to lure us away from God
and His precious Word. The devil wants to lead us into
the high mountains of earthly success and often promises us
quick recovery and health, longer life and fewer pains, if
we will do his bidding. But he always leads us away from
Christ. We must sell our soul's salvation for the few days
of health that the devil promises. In the days of sickness
we are especially in danger of listening to the enticing
promises of the devil. We must therefore daily seek the
Lord that He may keep us on the narrow way to life.
Nothing is of greater comfort therefore than to know that

the everlasting God, whose tender love moved Him to send His Son Jesus into the world to redeem us, will guide us with His eye in the paths of righteousness, where we live to His glory.

The Lord also leads us into the way eternal. Christ Jesus is the Way. In the days of sickness and affliction cults and isms of all kinds are brought to our attention, and in most glowing terms we are promised speedy recovery. In such days we need God that we may escape these cunnings and see the emptiness of the promises made to us. God must put a hedge about us to protect us against such false beliefs that rob us of our Savior from sin. Only by continuing faithfully in God's Word can we resist our tempters. Through the Word, God will show us and teach us the way in which we shall go.

Into our lives come seemingly strange happenings. Let us ever remember that God will guide us with His eye and instruct us in His truth and save us to the uttermost. Keeping this in mind, we shall never complain nor murmur as God leads us through trials and tribulations, because we know that, whatever way He guides us, He always brings us at last to our eternal home in heaven.

Prayer

In the hollow of Thine hand, Almighty God, hold me day after day. Whom shall I fear? Of whom shall I be afraid if Thou dost guide me with Thine eye? Every minute of the day I am in danger; but I fear no evil, for Thou art with me.

Put a hedge about me as sin lies at the door of my heart. Break Thou its power. Bind Satan and his host. Remove every doubt that assails me.

Be with all the loved ones of this home and keep them unharmed in body and soul. Our hearts would be heavy all the day if we did not know and believe that Thou dost uphold us. Forgive us all our sins. Keep our feet in the paths of righteousness and bring us at last into the many mansions which Christ Jesus has prepared for us. Amen.

Count Them One by One

And forget not all His benefits. — *Ps. 103, 2.*

The American world annually observes Thanksgiving Day. Can the shut-ins join in the hymns of praise to God? Most assuredly, even though they are sick abed and confined to their home by afflictions. Some blessings cannot be taken from us even though we are invalids. The greatest blessings belong to us always. David counts up the blessings that are ours as Christians; and when we remember these, we will sing hymns of praise unto our God.

The first among the blessings that we can count as ours is forgiveness. "Who forgiveth all thine iniquities." Forgiveness is ours through Christ. He has redeemed us, not with gold or silver, but with His holy, precious blood. This healing of the soul goes on day after day. Even though our body is sick unto death, it is well with the soul that has been forgiven and cleansed by the Great Physician.

The second blessing that is ours is healing of body and mind. "Who healeth all thy diseases." God is helping us day after day. Often we begin the day believing that we cannot live through it; but God always gives us sufficient strength to carry on. Every Christian shut-in must acknowledge this. That makes us cheerful and hopeful and removes morbid and distressing thoughts from our minds.

The third blessing that is ours is the assurance of God's guidance. "Who redeemeth thy life from destruction." Our life is not a matter of chance. Neither is life an accident. As we look back, we cannot fail to note that God has led and directed and guided us. He takes us by the hand and leads us. If He leads us, we always walk the narrow way that leads to life eternal.

As fourth blessing we enjoy the loving-kindness of God as well as the love of our fellow-men. "Who crowneth thee with loving-kindness and tender mercies." To enjoy the love and the friendship of those who are around us means a good deal in the day of sickness. If we had not a friend in the world, if not a soul cared whether we are sick or well, this life would be almost unbearable. But God has surrounded us with friends and loved ones and has put into their hearts the willingness to serve and to cheer and to help us.

As fifth blessing God gives us good things to eat. "Who satisfieth thy mouth with good things." He gives us food in great variety. He has not only given us bread and water, but fruits, meats, and vegetables. He has given us not only one kind of fruit, but has given us the pear, the apple, the orange. He has given us not only one kind of vegetables, but many. If our condition is such that we cannot eat the one, we can enjoy the other.

Thus, as we look about us, we shall find many blessings. Let us count up these blessings day after day, especially in the days when we feel downhearted and depressed. As we count them one by one, let us not forget to give thanks unto the Lord and praise Him with all our heart.

Prayer

I come to Thee mindful of Thy goodness, O Lord, and praise Thee day after day. Thy presence has been my strength. Thy love has been my joy. Thy forgiveness has filled me with peace. Thou hast opened Thy hand and showered upon me these many blessings. Make me truly grateful. Fill me with appreciation for every kind deed that friends and loved ones do for me. Teach me to be content in every condition and state of life. Bless my friends and loved ones day after day and keep us all faithful to Thee and to the Church of our Lord Jesus Christ, who has redeemed us and made us His own in His great, wonderful love. Amen.

God Cares

Consider the lilies of the field. — Matt. 6, 28.

Jesus took His sermons from practical life. Therefore He spoke in parables. He took a grain of wheat and compared it to the Word. He took a mustard-seed and likened its growth to the growth of the Christian Church. He pointed to the lilies of the field and taught lessons of God's providence. He took a little child and told us to have the same simple, yet genuine faith. Jesus tells us of some earthly incident and says that, because the earthly is true, therefore the heavenly is so much more true.

"If ye, then, being evil, know how to give good gifts unto your children, how much more shall your heavenly Father give the Holy Spirit to them that ask Him!" Parents give. They give wisely and generously. Love prompts them to give. No earthly parent would give a stone to a child that asks for bread nor a serpent when the child asks for a piece of meat. If a parent will not give anything harmful to his child, how much less will God do so! Therefore we should, when praying, confidently believe that God in His wisdom will give us those things that are beneficial to us.

"If God so clothe the grass of the field, which today is and tomorrow is cast into the oven, shall He not much more clothe you?" The grass is wonderfully made. It is beautiful. Not one blade is exactly like the other. But only too soon it withers. Now, if God takes care of the grass of the field, which tomorrow is cast into the oven, how much more will He provide for you! Therefore we should not worry, but trust in Him. With Paul we should say: "I have learned in whatsoever state I am therewith to be content," Phil. 4, 11.

"Which of you shall have an ass or an ox fallen into

a pit and will not straightway pull him out on the Sabbath-day?" said the Lord Jesus. Man is certainly better than an ox fallen into a pit; for Christ has given His life to redeem us from destruction. Because we have been redeemed, we can enter into fellowship with our heavenly Father. This assures us that God cares for us, even though many of our fellow-men ignore us and pass us by, unmindful of our needs and of our wants.

Let us thank God that we are more than an ox, more than the grass of the field, and more precious than the lilies. We are His children, whom He loves with such a wonderful love that nothing of the things present, nor the things to come, nor height, nor depth shall be able to separate us from this love of God, which is ours in Christ Jesus. Therefore we can trust in the Lord and know that He shall sustain us.

Prayer

Heavenly Father, I come to Thee as Thy child; for I have been redeemed by my Lord Jesus Christ, who has removed all my sins and reconciled me unto Thee. Lord, I come with all my burdens and cares, with all my troubles and pains, seeking relief and help from Thee. The anguish of my soul and the distress of my body are great. Truly, I am Thy child, and therefore I seek Thy peace and Thy help. If Thou shouldst mark sin, then, O Lord, I could not come. But there is forgiveness with Thee.

Let Thy almighty power heal me, if it be Thy will, that I may again worship Thee in Thy sanctuary and offer praise and thanks to Thee for Thy wonderful help. Show Thy mercy and Thy goodness to each one in this home and keep us all in that faith that brings us at last to the glory of the people of God. I ask it in Jesus' name. Amen.

Fie, Death!

But now is Christ risen from the dead and become the First-fruits of them that slept. — *1 Cor. 15, 20.*

The resurrection of Jesus is the crowning miracle of His life. Our Christian faith stands and falls with this fact, that Christ is risen from the dead. To deny the resurrection robs us of every hope and certainty of salvation. If Christ is not risen from the dead, then we need not look forward to an eternal life in heaven. To us, however, comes the glorious message, a historic fact which cannot be denied, that Christ is risen from the dead. We have in Christ, then, a living Savior. He is the Lord even over death. "Fie!" cried Cardinal Beaufort as he was told that he had but a few minutes to live. "Are my treasuries empty? Go, bribe death, bribe him." But death could not be bribed. The cardinal closed his eyes and was carried out to the grave. But death has been conquered. Christ has overcome death. He is a living Savior, who rules as the Lord of all over His people with tender love and turns everything to their good.

Jesus is a living Savior, and therefore we have forgiveness of all sins. Jesus took the guilt and blame of our sins upon Himself. Therefore He had to suffer the consequence of sin. The penalty of sin is death. So Jesus went to the cross and paid the debt with His holy, precious blood. But has He really accomplished that which He set out to do? His resurrection is the answer. When Christ rose from the dead, God proclaimed to the world that He had accepted Christ's sacrifice for our sins. Therefore all those who believe, enjoy a full cleansing and are acquitted in the just courts of God. That is why we rejoice as Christians in the resurrection of Jesus.

Jesus is the living Savior, and therefore we have the promise of life eternal. As we stand at open graves, Jesus tells us: "I am the Resurrection and the Life; he that believeth in Me, though he were dead, yet shall he live," John 11, 25. As you and I face death, Jesus gives us the blessed assurance: "Because I live, ye shall live also," John 14, 19.

Our faith, then, rests upon this firm foundation: Jesus is risen from the dead. Therefore we need not be ashamed of the Gospel, for it is a power of God unto salvation to every one that believeth. We need not be afraid of the Judgment of God, for our sin has been canceled through the blood of Jesus Christ. We need not be afraid of the terrors of death, for heaven is our home. Even in the days of sickness and affliction we can join the multitude of Christian men and women with the confident hope that Christ is with us alway and that life eternal is ours by God's wonderful grace, because Christ Jesus is risen from the dead.

Prayer

Lord Jesus, Lover of my soul, Thou art my ever-living Savior, in whom I put my trust. Abide with me. Dwell within my heart and my home and let Thy divine presence be with me day after day that peace and joy may fill my heart and mind. Amid my trials, troubles, and afflictions teach me to know and to believe that the suffering of this present world is but passing and that we have no abiding city here on earth, but have an eternal home with Thee, in which there is fulness of joy forever. Keep us all steadfast in this faith unto the end. Forgive us where we have doubted Thee and Thy promises. Cleanse us from every sin with which we have offended Thee. Fill us all with good cheer and hope and bring us at last redeemed into Thy kingdom, where Thou, as the ever-living Savior, wilt abide with all Thy saints forevermore. Amen.

Jesus and You

Lo, I am with you alway. — *Matt. 28, 20.*

To travel alone along the road of trouble and sickness is a discouraging task and often ends in despair. We need help and strength from without. Christ promises us strength and help. "Lo, I am with you alway." He is our Companion in our daily struggles and strife and sickness. With Him we can commune in prayer. He speaks to us through His written Word. With Him we can hopefully and cheerfully and patiently look ahead.

Depressed, Jesus will make you a hopeful Christian, filled with confidence. Christ Jesus will not let you sink in the troubled waters, but will reach out His hands and lift you up, saying, "Be not afraid; I am with thee."

Weeping, Jesus will make you a comforted Christian. There are many tears. Jesus wipes away these tears, telling us of the many mansions which He has prepared for us in heaven. We all stand at open graves into which we have laid some loved one. How empty is life! Jesus comes to us with this blessed assurance: "Because I live, ye shall live also." What a glorious promise! What a hopeful outlook! Heaven is ours, where there are no more tears. Heaven is our home, where there are no more heartaches. Heaven is our abiding city, where we shall dwell forever with the Lord in the fulness of joy.

Sin-stained, Jesus will make of you a forgiven saint. Trouble and sickness bring sins to our remembrance. Ofttimes a voice whispers within that we are being punished for our sins and deserve to be afflicted. In such hours our sins rise like monsters, and our accusing conscience tells us that these sins are too many and too great to be forgiven. Christ Jesus comes to you with the blessed assurance that He will blot out all transgressions with His holy, precious blood and remember them no more. Thus the child of

God is indeed not perfect, but has a perfect Savior, who forgives all sins and brings into our hearts peace and hope and certainty. Cleansed, the sinner becomes a saint.

This is the blessed assurance that comes to us day after day from our Lord Jesus Christ. His divine presence in our daily life guarantees to us these promises. Christ in our lives, in our homes, and in our hearts makes us look forward hopefully, enabling us to bear our cross cheerfully and patiently.

Prayer

Abide with me, blessed Savior, throughout this day. I need Thee, I need Thee every moment of the day. Thou art acquainted with my troubles and my pain. My sins are also known unto Thee. Thou art acquainted with all my ways, and not a thought is hidden from Thee. Yet Thou dost love me and hast promised to give me strength and help. O Lord, if it were not for these promises, I should sink into despair. Lift Thou me up and set me upon a rock and let me cling to Thee. Forgive me every sin and give me grace to bear patiently the burdens laid upon me.

Give strength to us all to believe that Thou art with us alway, the unseen Friend ever present to help us and to bless us with peace and forgiveness. Lead us safely through the storms of life into Thy eternal presence. Amen.

The Rock Higher than I

Behold, I lay in Zion for a foundation a Stone, a tried Stone.
Is. 28, 16.

Christ is the Corner-stone of every Christian life. The Christian builds upon Jesus as the certain and sure foundation of his faith. Throughout the ages the Christian world has found in Christ a rock which towers over the wrecks of time. Kingdoms have come and gone, but Christ and His Word abide. Therefore Isaiah says that He is "a tried Stone."

Every human being needs to build upon such a firm foundation if his soul is not to go down in hopeless despair. Only if we stand upon this Rock of Ages, can we find peace against the accusing conscience, hope in the hour of death, and comfort in the day of trouble. Jesus is the only sure Rock and tried Foundation-stone. On the cross He has satisfied the justice of God and paid the penalty for our sin with His own blood. Therefore He is our peace, and in Him we find perfect salvation.

Christ removes from our hearts the fear of death and of the Judgment to come. He goes with us through the valley of the shadow of death as Companion and Friend. He takes us by the hand and leads us to heaven.

Christ is also the Strength of our life and our Stay in trouble. "Hast thou not known, hast thou not heard, that the everlasting God, the Lord, the Creator of the ends of the earth, fainteth not, neither is weary? They that wait upon the Lord shall renew their strength," Is. 40, 28. 31.

Whatever may come to pass in our lives, whatever may confront us today, of this we can be certain, that Christ is with us and that He is able to help. Therefore you and I can with confidence look ahead even in the days of sickness and say: Christ will help me; He is the tried and tested Stone, upon which I can build for time and eternity.

Prayer

Lord Jesus, Thou art the Rock that is higher than I, to which I flee as the troubled waters surround me. Lo, I sink unless Thou wilt reach out Thine hand to uphold me. I know that Thou wilt not forsake me.

Often I have left Thee in my folly and pride. But today I realize, O Lord, that I cannot go on without Thee. Forgive me all my sins and transgressions and by Thy gentle hand lead me again into the paths of righteousness. Restore my soul to Thy grace and keep me steadfast and true unto the end. I ask this of Thee, who hast loved me even unto death. Amen.

A Handful of Everlastings

We have also a more sure word of prophecy, whereunto ye do well that ye take heed. — *2 Pet. 1, 19.*

Our faith is built upon the sure foundation of the Word of God. This Word is not a gathering of cunning fables and pet theories of men. The Scriptures have been given to us by inspiration. They are God's message to man. If there is a God, — and who doubts it? — then He must have revealed Himself to mankind from the beginning. Here is a Book that was begun in the childhood of the world and from beginning to end claims that it comes from God. Its wonderful message of forgiveness and its promises of eternal life are so divine and convincing that we cannot doubt its claim.

These Scriptures give us the most glorious promises and fill us with hope and cheer as we journey along life's road.

Have you trouble? This Word tells you: "Seek ye the Lord while He may be found; call ye upon Him while He is near," Is. 55, 6.

Are you worried? The Scriptures say: "Commit thy way unto the Lord; trust also in Him; and He shall bring it to pass," Ps. 37, 5.

Is sin vexing you? Then hear the wonderful promise of God: "I, even I, am He that blotteth out thy transgressions for Mine own sake and will not remember thy sins," Is. 43, 25.

Are you looking for peace? Jesus comes to you, saying: "Peace I leave with you, My peace I give unto you; not as the world giveth, give I unto you. Let not your heart be troubled, neither let it be afraid," John 14, 27.

Are you looking for cheer? The Bible offers it to you on many pages. "Rejoice in the Lord alway; and again I say, Rejoice," Phil. 4, 4.

Are you weary? Jesus stretches out His hands to you

and invites you to come to Him: "Come unto Me, all ye that labor and are heavy laden, and I will give you rest. Take My yoke upon you and learn of Me; for I am meek and lowly in heart, and ye shall find rest unto your souls. For My yoke is easy, and My burden is light," Matt. 11, 28—30.

Thus we can go again and again to this Word and through it strengthen our faith. Therefore, amid all perplexing problems and trying sufferings let us seek refuge in these Scriptures, which are sure and certain, the eternal Word of God. If we do take heed of them, it will be well with our souls, and we can hopefully and courageously look into the future, knowing that there is safety and salvation in our Lord.

Prayer

Great is Thy name, and mighty is Thy help, O Lord. Therefore I come to Thee. Thou hast promised to watch over me with Thy tender care and to uphold me in Thy loving mercy. Thou hast given me the blessed promise to be with me whithersoever I go. Nothing is hidden from Thee. Thou knowest my downsitting and my uprising, Thou understandest my thoughts afar off. Thou hast wonderfully made me and hast graciously preserved me. Let my lips and my heart praise Thee for this Thy goodness.

Wherever I have grieved Thee with my sins and offended Thee with my doubts and unbelief, forgive. Teach me to trust in Thee and rely upon Thy strength. Give to us all who dwell in this Christian home a greater faith and a deeper love for Thee. Keep us faithful to the end, until we shall stand in Thy presence, in the fulness of Thy eternal joy. Hear my petitions for Jesus' sake, who daily makes intercessions for me at Thy throne. Amen.

Name of Wondrous Love

And thou shalt call His name Jesus: for He shall save His people from their sins. — *Matt. 1, 21.*

Jesus is the Lord's human name. It is the most wondrous name in the world. Jesus is the same as the Old Testament name Joshua. Joshua led the children of Israel into the Promised Land, Jesus, our Joshua, leads us into the promised land of heaven. Jesus means Savior. "For He shall save His people from their sins." "There is none other name under heaven given among men whereby we must be saved," Acts 4, 12. Other names may mean much to us. We hold in high esteem the names of Washington, Jefferson, and Lincoln. None of these, however, can save us from sin. We can and do admire these men. But they can never be to us what Jesus is.

Jesus transforms our lives. Jesus does not merely reform, but He transforms us. He takes us out of the empire of Satan and makes us citizens of God's kingdom. Jesus made the publican Matthew into an apostle; the persecuting Paul, into a zealous missionary; the sinning woman, into a weeping penitent. Truly, there is no more wondrous name in the world than the name of Jesus.

This Jesus comes also to you and saves you from sin. He is your Stay in trouble and your Companion in sickness. He alone can lighten your burden, remove your sins, and fill you with the hope of eternal life.

Prayer

O Lord Jesus, I come to Thee, the Friend of sinners and the Lover of my soul. Thou didst bear the burden of my iniquity upon the cross and hast finished salvation for me. Let me ever praise and thank Thee for this wonderful sacrifice of love through which Thou hast brought forgiveness and peace to my heart. Grant that I may ever look to the Cross for healing and also learn to bear patiently the afflictions of life, even as Thou patiently didst meet Thy suffering on the cross. Take me by Thy hand and lead me into the paths of righteousness. Make Thy presence known to us all and create in us new hearts, hearts that will love Thee and serve Thee now and forever. Amen.

The Uplifting Christ

And I, if I be lifted up from the earth, will draw all men unto Me. — *John 12, 32.*

All mankind needs food, clothing, and shelter. But these are not man's greatest needs. True, they are very essential. But they profit us nothing if we lose our soul. This soul can be saved alone through Jesus Christ. Therefore He seeks to draw all men unto Himself. In Him we find life eternal. Jesus, however, must be lifted up to the cross to help us. Only the uplifted Christ, who has shed His blood for the sins of the world, has power to save. Only by His substitutionary death on the cross has He freed us from the terrors and fears of death.

Those who look to the uplifted Christ find forgiveness, peace, and hope. This forgiveness, peace, and hope makes us cheerful amid the trials and troubles of this world. If we look to Christ, who has saved us for all eternity, we shall realize that the sufferings of this present life are but for a short time. Then comes the glory. In that glory there shall be no more pain, and there shall be no more death.

The uplifted Christ has cleansed us through His precious blood from our sins, and therefore we are certain of eternal life. Knowing that heaven is our home should help us overcome our disappointments and worries and cares. Knowing that Christ Jesus went to the cross and suffered greater pain than we can ever suffer in this world should make us patient and willing to bear our burdens.

In the days of trouble and affliction we draw closer to

Him who has redeemed us. If He has saved our soul, then
He will certainly also watch over our body in this world.
He will be with us every hour of the day and through
the long night-watches. In the uplifted Christ we then
have forgiveness and comfort, we receive strength and
help, and through Him learn patiently to carry our cross
after Him.

Prayer

Draw me unto Thee, gracious Savior, with Thy divine love
and keep me unto the end of days at the foot of the cross, where
there is healing and forgiveness. Thou knowest that Satan ever
seeks to fill me with doubt or to entice me to go up into the high
mountains to behold the glory of the world and to live for this
life only. Grant me strength to resist these allurements and to
overcome every temptation that comes into my life. Thou canst
preserve me from every evil of body and soul. Give Thy holy
angels charge over me to keep me in all Thy ways that I may
come at last into Thy presence, to dwell in the fulness of Thy joy.

In Thy mercy preserve us all and keep us faithful to Thy
Word that we may ever remember that we can profit nothing if
we gain the whole world and thereby lose our soul. Forgive us
all our sins and keep us in Thy saving grace. I ask this of Thee
who hast loved me unto death, even the death on the cross. Amen.

Our Glorious Hope

If in this life only we have hope in Christ, we are of all men
most miserable. — *1 Cor. 15, 19.*

Hope is the mainspring of life. Take hope out of our
lives, and we have no peace. We are driven into despair.

Even those who ignore God have hope in this world;
they hope to make a living; they hope to see better days;
they hope to get well.

Nothing fills us with greater hope than the resurrection
of Jesus Christ. This resurrection of Jesus tells us that He
is God and that therefore His Word and His promises
are true. Jesus has promised to be with us alway. He

has promised to send us the Comforter. He has assured us that we shall live because He lives.

At no other time in life do we need these promises as much as when we are shut in by affliction and sickness. These promises assure us that we are never alone. We have the abiding presence of the Lord Jesus Christ.

But we have another hope given us through the resurrection of Jesus. His resurrection tells us that Christ is our Savior. The Father delared, by raising Christ from the dead, that He had accepted Jesus' sacrifice as full, complete payment for our sins. Jesus has crushed the Serpent's head. He has won the victory over Satan. Therefore we can look hopefully into the future, knowing that nothing can condemn us as long as we are hid in Christ.

Since Christ has risen from the dead, we also have this hope, that our afflicted, sickly body shall rise in incorruption and be like unto the glorious body of our Lord Jesus Christ. In this world we have many trials. We Christians suffer the same pains and aches as do people who ignore Christ and deny Him. If only in this world we have hope, we are of all men most miserable. But our hope is this, that beyond the grave this suffering body will rise in perfection. All tears shall be wiped away from our eyes. There shall be no more pain. There shall be no more death. In the presence of the Lord there is fulness of joy forevermore. So our hope takes us beyond this life into endless eternity. All this is made certain and sure by the resurrection of Jesus.

Easter, then, brings to us the most blessed joy and the most hopeful message in the world. We can truly say with Paul: "I reckon that the sufferings of this present time are not worthy to be compared with the glory which shall be revealed in us," Rom. 8, 18. And we can also full of confidence add: "For our light affliction, which is but for a moment, worketh for us a far more exceeding and eternal weight of glory; while we look not at things which are seen, but at things which are not seen; for the things which are seen are temporal, but the things which are not seen are eternal," 2 Cor. 4, 17. 18.

Prayer

Lord Jesus, ever-living Savior, I praise Thee because Thou hast overcome sin and death and hast given to me forgiveness and peace, which is assured to me by Thy glorious resurrection from the dead. Show me Thy mercy also today and blot out all my sins. In my suffering, pain, and affliction I look to Thee, filled with the ever-living hope that Thou wilt set me free from the bondage of sin and its suffering for all eternity. Give me grace to believe that Thou art very near to me and comfort me with the glorious Gospel every hour of the day.

Keep us all steadfast in Thy Word and faith unto the end and bring us at last into the glory that awaits the people of God. Hear us for Thy name's sake. Amen.

Four Great Truths

God speaks to us in the Bible. As He speaks, He is concerned about one thing, the salvation of our souls. Therefore He has made known four great truths that man may learn that he is a sinner saved by grace.

1. Man is a law-breaker, having transgressed the holy will of God as revealed in the Ten Commandments and summed up by Jesus Christ in the words: "Thou shalt love the Lord, thy God, with all thy heart, and with all thy soul, and with all thy mind. Thou shalt love thy neighbor as thyself," Matt. 22, 37. 39. Therefore man is worthy of death, which is the penalty for sin. "The soul that sinneth, it shall die," Ezek. 18, 20. "The wages of sin is death," Rom. 6, 23. "There is not a just man upon earth, that doeth good and sinneth not," Eccl. 7, 20.

2. No man can save himself. "Not by works of righteousness which we have done, but according to His mercy He saved us," Titus 3, 5. "If by grace, then is it no more of works," Rom. 11, 6. "We are all as an unclean thing, and all our righteousnesses are as filthy rags," Is. 64, 6.

3. Jesus, in our place and for us, has made full, complete atonement, paying for all our sins by shedding His holy, precious blood and dying on the cross. "He was wounded for our transgressions, He was bruised for our iniquities; the chastisement of our peace was upon Him, and by His stripes we are healed," Is. 53, 5. "Christ His own self bare our sins in His own body on the tree that we, being dead to sins, should live unto righteousness; by whose stripes ye were healed," 1 Pet. 2, 24. "Behold the Lamb of God, which taketh away the sin of the world," John 1, 29.

4. We must accept the Lord Jesus Christ as our personal Savior from sin by believing on Him. "Believe on the Lord Jesus Christ, and thou shalt be saved," Acts 16, 31. "God so loved the world that He gave His only-begotten Son, that whosoever believeth in Him should not perish, but have everlasting life," John 3, 16. The believer is therefore daily forgiven. "The blood of Jesus Christ, His Son, cleanseth us from all sin," 1 John 1, 7.

This in a few words tells you the all-essential truths of the Scriptures which hold out hope to every one.

Prayer

Lord, Thy Word is truth. In this Word Thou hast made known unto me Thy wonderful grace. Let Thy Holy Spirit fill me with a faith that will accept without wavering these Thy revelations. I am unworthy of this truth; for I indeed have often sinned against Thee. I have no power nor strength within me to cling to Thy Word. Thou must create this faith in me through Thy Holy Spirit, and Thou must keep me steadfast unto the end. Accept me just as I am. I have nothing to bring. I have no virtues that can make me acceptable in Thy sight. I plead for mercy in Jesus' name. Let His precious blood wash me and purge me. Grant that the Lamb of God that taketh away the sin of the world also may take away mine in mercy and give me peace. I ask this because of Him who has given His life that I may come to the foot of the cross and find healing — Jesus, my Lord. Amen.

What Can the Shut-ins Do?

"Lord, what wilt Thou have me to do?" — Acts 9, 6.

Sometimes those who are shut in for months wonder what they can do for the Lord Jesus Christ and His Christian Church. They are denied the privilege of coming to the Lord's house to worship and join in the fellowship with Christian people, to praise and glorify and confess Christ publicly. These shut-ins are not in a position to work in the Kingdom and because of their affliction not even able to make sacrifices for Christ and His Church.

Yet these shut-ins have an opportunity to serve the Lord. They are given a great privilege and are in duty bound to do their part — they can pray. The shut-ins can give themselves to prayer at the time of the church services. They can pour out their hearts to God and beseech Him to bless the message of His Word and to give to those who are assembled receptive hearts, so that this Word will not fall upon stony ground. Every shut-in knows of some one who is unchurched or growing careless, and for such he or she can especially pray, pleading that God may move their hearts that they will go to church and hear the message of instruction or warning or comfort. If all shut-ins give themselves to much prayer, they will accomplish mighty things. God has promised to answer such petitions.

When shut-ins therefore feel as though they cannot do much for the Lord, let this be their comfort, that through their prayer they can be a real strength and help to their

church, its members, and to the pastor. We serve the
Lord not only when like Paul we go to the ends of the
earth to preach the Gospel, but also when in the quiet of
our sick-room we daily and fervently pray.

Prayer

Lord Jesus, King of kings and Lord of lords, I worship Thee
as my Lord and God. Thy name is most wondrous. There is
none like unto Thee. All things are in Thy power, and Thou
dost answer prayer. The universe is Thine and with the Father
and the Holy Spirit Thou dost rule all things. Day after day
I behold Thy power. Thou canst move the desires of men to do
Thy will. Therefore I beseech Thee, O gracious Lord, that Thou
wouldst send many, and especially those whom I know and love,
to Thy sanctuary that they may hear Thy Word. Grant that my
pastor especially will say just those things that are needful for
those who hear him, that they may come to the knowledge of
their sins and seek forgiveness with Thee. Thou hast also redeemed them with Thy precious blood. Let Thy healing hand
cleanse their conscience, strengthen their faith, and comfort their
hearts. Wondrous Savior, let Thy name be known unto the ends
of the earth, so that everywhere mankind may confess and accept
Thee, to the glory of Thy wondrous name. Amen.

Bearing Burdens

Bear ye one another's burdens and so fulfil the law of Christ.
Gal. 6, 2.

We are social creatures. We are born into families and
therefore are dependent upon one another. As babes we
must rely altogether upon the good will of our parents.
For years they must nourish us, clothe us, and take care
of our every need. Even as youths we lack judgment and
tact, and therefore our parents must guide and direct us.
In the days of sickness we must be taken care of by those
who are in the home. No one can live so utterly alone as

completely to ignore every other person in the world, least of all those of his own household.

Selfishness therefore is outlawed by the Scriptures. "Bear ye one another's burdens." That is the law of Christ. The Christian religion is a religion of sacrifice. Christ Himself bore our own sins on the tree and therewith made the greatest sacrifice in the world. Only because He was wounded for our transgressions and bore our griefs, are we at peace with God, fully reconciled, and saved.

Christ's sacrifice should teach us the lesson of sacrifice and service. We should ever be ready to bear one another's burdens. Wherever possible, we should lighten the cares of others and take the load from off their shoulders.

Bearing one another's burdens is not limited to any group of people. Of course, we should first of all take care of those of our own family and then of those of the household of faith, our fellow-Christians. But as we go along the Jericho road of life, we should be ever ready to help any one who is suffering and troubled and distressed. Every one who needs our help and our love is our neighbor, and by helping all who are in distress, we fulfil the law of Christ.

Prayer

Lord, heavenly Father, Thou knowest our weaknesses and shortcomings. Thou art acquainted with all our ways. Too often, we confess, O Lord, we are selfish and self-centered, looking only after our own comforts and our own ease. Lord, forgive us these our sins through Jesus Christ. Teach us to look up to the cross day after day to behold how Christ has given His life that we might have salvation. Grant that our hearts may grow tender in love as the needs of others cry out to us, the needs of their body as well as the needs of their soul. Grant also, heavenly Father, that we in this home, each and every one, may be ready and willing unselfishly to serve the other. We ask this in Jesus' name. Amen.

TEACH ME TO PRAY

Morning Prayer

I thank Thee, heavenly Father, through Jesus Christ, my Savior, because of Thy wonderful protection given me this night. I ask Thee to be with me today, protecting me from all dangers and guarding me against the snares of sin. Lead me into ways acceptable to Thee. Thou knowest that I am pursued by sin and am helpless in my own strength. Therefore I come to Thee, heavenly Father, in this morning hour, seeking Thy divine help. Strengthen Thou my faith, protect my body, and shield my soul. I place myself into Thy divine care. Let Thy holy angels surround me, so that Satan and sin may have no power over me. Amen.

Evening Prayer

I thank Thee, good and gracious heavenly Father, through Jesus Christ that Thou hast been with me all through the day. Forgive because of Jesus Christ every sin which I have done this day in thought, word, and deed and mercifully protect me and all my loved ones this night, that no harm or danger may come near us.

Therefore I place myself into Thy hands, both my body and my soul, asking that Thou wouldst send Thy holy angels to watch over me. Protect all those who trust in Thee and bring us at last to that eternal day in heaven, for Jesus' sake. Amen.

Prayer before an Operation

O Lord, the hour has come that I must face this serious operation. Fear wants to grip my heart, anxious thoughts possess me. Whither shall I turn to find peace and calm? I know of no other place in the world but at Thy throne.

Therefore I come, O Lord, I come. Give me to understand and know that Thou wilt not forsake me, but art watching over my life when I am in the deep sleep. Remove every fear from my heart. Let me trust in Thee.

Guide the surgeon's hand and give him understanding and wisdom. Let the fear of the Lord also dwell in his heart. Bless the nurses who take care of me.

Lord, every sin which I have committed, forgive. They have been many, and today they come to my remembrance. But my hope is built upon Jesus Christ and His blood. Let His blood cleanse me from every evil thought that has passed through my heart, every evil word that I have spoken, and every sinful deed that I have done.

And now, O Lord, I am at peace with Thee, for Thy forgiveness is in my heart. In Thee I trust in this hour. Be Thou my Staff and Rod. Keep me in Thy grace for Jesus' sake. Amen.

Prayer after an Operation

Lord God, I will bless Thee forever and ever, for Thou hast wondrously preserved my life when I was at the brink of death. Thou hast steadied the surgeon's hand and given him wisdom and understanding. Thy wonderful grace has led me safely through this danger.

Lord, I thank Thee for this Thy goodness and ask that Thou wouldst continue to bless me and let Thy healing hand rest upon me, that I may speedily return home to my loved ones, fully recovered and strengthened.

Merciful Father, grant that my thanksgiving and praise will not be a passing emotion, but continue to express itself through consecrated service to Thee. Thou hast given me a new lease upon life. Thou art adding to the length of my days. Give me grace to remember that Thou hast upheld me and grant that with deeper devotion I may study Thy Word and with greater zeal worship Thee in Thy sanctuary. Let my lips be full of praise.

Give me strength to confess to all mankind that Thou art a very present Help in trouble, that all may know that Thy promises are true. Keep me steadfast in Thy Word and preserve me unto the end of days in that one faith which is in Christ Jesus, my Lord. Amen.

"BRING THE BOOK"
Nehemiah 8, 1
DAILY BIBLE-READINGS FOR SHUT-INS

1. John 14, 1—6	11. John 3, 14—17	21. Rev. 22, 16—21
2. Luke 11, 1—13	12. Mark 4, 36—41	22. 2 Cor. 12, 7—9
3. Phil. 4, 6—13	13. Rom. 8, 26—39	23. Luke 23, 39—43
4. Rom. 5, 1—11	14. Eph. 2, 8—14	24. Heb. 11, 23—26
5. Matt. 11, 25—30	15. 2 Tim. 4, 1—8	25. John 10, 7—11
6. 1 Cor. 13, 4—13	16. 1 John 1, 5—10	26. John 10, 27. 28
7. Jas. 5, 13—20	17. Rev. 7, 9—17	27. 1 Cor. 15, 14—20
8. Heb. 12, 2—14	18. Acts 16, 25—33	28. 1 Cor. 15, 55—58
9. Matt. 8, 1—13	19. 2 Pet. 1, 19—21	29. Luke 17, 11—19
10. Rom. 3, 20—24	20. John 15, 1—5	30. John 21, 15—19

1. Luke 15, 1—10	12. John 15, 13—17	22. John 14, 15—19
2. Luke 15, 11—24	13. Eph. 6, 10—19	23. Titus 3, 4—8
3. John 6, 35—40	14. John 1, 29—34	24. Matt. 26, 36—46
4. Rom. 1, 16. 17	15. Matt. 17, 1—8	25. Heb. 10, 22—25
5. 2 Pet. 3, 8—18	16. Luke 18, 35—43	26. 1 Tim. 2, 1—8
6. 1 Tim. 6, 20. 21	17. Luke 19, 1—10	27. John 11, 21—29
7. Luke 22, 31—35	18. Rom. 11, 33—36	28. 2 Cor. 6, 14—18
8. 1 John 4, 11—19	19. John 16, 22—24	29. Col. 3, 15—17
9. Rom. 10, 9—17	20. 1 Tim. 1, 15—17	30. John 6, 66—69
10. Heb. 13, 5—16	21. Rev. 3, 14—22	31. Luke 24, 13—29
11. Heb. 13, 18—21		

1. Ps. 23	9. Ps. 40	17. Ps. 103	24. Ps. 145
2. Ps. 4	10. Ps. 42	18. Ps. 119, 1—16	25. Is. 40, 1—10
3. Ps. 19	11. Ps. 46	19. Ps. 119, 97—112	26. Is. 53
4. Ps. 25	12. Ps. 51	20. Ps. 121	27. Is. 54, 4—10
5. Ps. 27	13. Ps. 73	21. Ps. 122	28. Is. 55
6. Ps. 31	14. Ps. 84	22. Ps. 130	29. Is. 64, 1—8
7. Ps. 32	15. Ps. 90	23. Ps. 139	30. Ps. 150
8. Ps. 34	16. Ps. 91		

TEXTUAL INDEX

www.ingramcontent.com/pod-product-compliance
Lightning Source LLC
Chambersburg PA
CBHW021242090426
42740CB00006B/645